First Men, America's Presidents Series

Gerald Ford
The All-American President

FIRST MEN, AMERICA'S PRESIDENTS SERIES
BARBARA BENNETT PETERSON – SERIES EDITOR
OREGON STATE UNIVERSITY, USA

Citizen Lincoln
Ward M. McAfee
2004. ISBN: 1-59454-112-4
(Hardcover)
2008. ISBN: 978-1-60456-628-4
(Softcover)

**Theodore Roosevelt:
A Political Life**
Thomas Lansford
2004. ISBN: 978-1-59033-990-8

**John Quincy Adams:
Yankee Nationalist**
Paul E. Teed
2005. ISBN: 978-1-59454-797-1
(Hardcover)
2010. ISBN: 978-1-60876-914-8
(Softcover)
2010. ISBN: 978-1-61761-172-8
(E-Book)

**George Washington, America's
Moral Exemplar**
Barbara Bennett Peterson
2005. ISBN: 978-1-59454-230-9
(Hardcover)
2011. ISBN: 978-1-61761-678-5
(Softcover)

President James K. Polk
Louise Mayo
2006. ISBN: 978-1-59454-718-1

**Franklin Delano Roosevelt,
Preserver of Spirit and Hope**
Barbara Bennett Peterson
2006. ISBN: 978-1-60021-117-8
(Hardcover)
2008. ISBN: 978-1-60456-496-9
(Softcover)
2008. ISBN: 978-1-61209-734-3
(E-Book)

**Benjamin Harrison:
Centennial President**
*Anne Chieko Moore (Author)
Anne Hale (Editor)*
2006. ISBN: 1-60021-066-X
(Hardcover)
2009. ISBN: 978-1-60456-330-6
(Softcover)
2009. ISBN: 978-1-61728-668-1
(E-Book)

**Chester Alan Arthur:
The Life of a Gilded Age
Politician and President**
Gregory J. Dehler
2007. ISBN: 978-1-60021-079-1
(Hardcover and Softcover)

In the Shadow of the Great Rebellion: The Life of Andrew Johnson, Seventeenth President of the United States (1808-1875)
G.L. Donhardt (Editor)
2007. ISBN: 978-1-60021-086-4
(Hardcover)
2007. ISBN: 978-1-60456-944-5
(Softcover)

William Henry Harrison: General and President
Mary Jane Child Queen
2007. ISBN: 1-60021-407-X

President Herbert Hoover
Donald W. Whisenhunt
2007. ISBN: 978-1-60021-476-2
(Hardcover)
2008. ISBN: 978-1-60456-382-5
(Softcover)

President Zachary Taylor: The Hero President
Elbert B. Smith
2007. ISBN: 978-1-60021-602-1
(Hardcover)
2010. ISBN: 978-1-60876-912-4
(Softcover)
2010. ISBN: 978-1-61761-173-5
(E-Book)

Woodrow Wilson: The Last Romantic
Mary Stockwell,
2008. ISBN: 978-1-60021-815-6

John Tyler: A Rare Career
Lyle Nelson
2008. ISBN: 978-1-60021-961-6
(Hardcover)
2011. ISBN: 978-1-61761-668-6
(Softcover)

Thomas Jefferson: A Public Life, A Private Life
David Kiracofe
2008. ISBN: 978-1-60456-061-9
(Hardcover)
2011. ISBN: 978-1-61761-679-2
(Softcover)

Martin Van Buren: The Little Magician
Pierre-Marie Loizeau
2008. ISBN: 978-1-60456-773-1
(Hardcover)
2011. ISBN: 978-1-61761-781-2
(Softcover)
2008. ISBN: 978-1-61668-054-1
(E-Book)

James Madison: Defender of the American Republic
Donald Dewey
and Barbara Bennett Peterson
2009. ISBN: 978-1-60456-858-5
(Hardcover)
2011. ISBN: 978-1-61761-669-3
(Softcover)

Andrew Jackson in Context
Matthew Warshauer
2009. ISBN: 978-1-60741-709-5

John F. Kennedy: The New Frontier President
David L. Snead (Author)
Barbara Bennett Peterson (Editor)
2010. ISBN: 978-1-61668-925-4
(Hardcover)
2010. ISBN: 978-1-61209-074-0
(E-Book)

Chester Alan Arthur: The Life of a Gilded Age Politician and President
Gregory J. Dehler
2010. ISBN: 978-1-60876-913-1

William H. Taft
Richard G. Frederick
2010. ISBN: 978-1-60876-917-9
(Hardcover)
2010. ISBN: 978-1-61668-821-9
(E-Book)

The Presidency of Grover Cleveland
Joel D. Benson
2010. ISBN: 978-1-60876-974-2

President James K. Polk
Louise Mayo
2011. ISBN: 978-1-61122-785-7
(Softcover)
2011 ISBN: 978-1-61122-222-7
(E-Book)

Jimmy Carter: Politician with Principles
Michael T. Ruddy
2011. ISBN: 978-1-61761-850-5
(Hardcover)
2011. ISBN: 978-1-61122-213-5
(E-Book)

William McKinley: A Modern Man
Deborah R. Marinski
2011. ISBN: 978-1-61122-812-0

Dwight D. Eisenhower: An American Icon
*Robert E. Dewhirst
and Matthew A. Johnson*
2011. ISBN: 978-1-61122-814-4

Andrew Jackson in Context
Matthew Warshauer
2011. ISBN: 978-1-61209-622-3
(Softcover)
2009. ISBN: 978-1-61209-595-0
(E-Book)

Gerald R. Ford: The All-American President
Brian E. Birdnow
2011. ISBN: 978-1-61209-670-4

George H.W. Bush: In Defense of Principle
Wesley B. Borucki
2011. ISBN: 978-1-61122-133-6
(Hardcover)
2011. ISBN: 978-1-61122-429-0
(E-Book)

FIRST MEN, AMERICA'S PRESIDENTS SERIES

GERALD FORD
THE ALL-AMERICAN PRESIDENT

BRIAN E. BIRDNOW

Nova Science Publishers, Inc.
New York

Copyright © 2011 by Nova Science Publishers, Inc.

All rights reserved. No part of this book may be reproduced, stored in a retrieval system or transmitted in any form or by any means: electronic, electrostatic, magnetic, tape, mechanical photocopying, recording or otherwise without the written permission of the Publisher.

For permission to use material from this book please contact us:
Telephone 631-231-7269; Fax 631-231-8175
Web Site: http://www.novapublishers.com

NOTICE TO THE READER

The Publisher has taken reasonable care in the preparation of this book, but makes no expressed or implied warranty of any kind and assumes no responsibility for any errors or omissions. No liability is assumed for incidental or consequential damages in connection with or arising out of information contained in this book. The Publisher shall not be liable for any special, consequential, or exemplary damages resulting, in whole or in part, from the readers' use of, or reliance upon, this material. Any parts of this book based on government reports are so indicated and copyright is claimed for those parts to the extent applicable to compilations of such works.

Independent verification should be sought for any data, advice or recommendations contained in this book. In addition, no responsibility is assumed by the publisher for any injury and/or damage to persons or property arising from any methods, products, instructions, ideas or otherwise contained in this publication.

This publication is designed to provide accurate and authoritative information with regard to the subject matter covered herein. It is sold with the clear understanding that the Publisher is not engaged in rendering legal or any other professional services. If legal or any other expert assistance is required, the services of a competent person should be sought. FROM A DECLARATION OF PARTICIPANTS JOINTLY ADOPTED BY A COMMITTEE OF THE AMERICAN BAR ASSOCIATION AND A COMMITTEE OF PUBLISHERS.

Additional color graphics may be available in the e-book version of this book.

LIBRARY OF CONGRESS CATALOGING-IN-PUBLICATION DATA

Birdnow, Brian E.
 Gerald R. Ford : the all-American president / Brian E. Birdnow.
   p. cm.
 Includes bibliographical references and index.
 ISBN 978-1-61209-670-4 (hardcover)
 1. Ford, Gerald R., 1913-2006. 2. Presidents--United States--Biography.
3. United States--Politics and government--1969-1974. 4. United
States--Politics and government--1974-1977. I. Title.
 E866.B57 2011
 973.925092--dc22
 [B]
                              2011002543

Published by Nova Science Publishers, Inc. † New York

Contents

Preface		ix
Acknowledgments		xi
Foreword		xiii
Chapter 1	Main Traveled Roads	1
Chapter 2	Hail to the Victors	9
Chapter 3	America First?	21
Chapter 4	The Distinguished Gentleman from Michigan	35
Chapter 5	Moving on Up: 1961-1972	51
Chapter 6	Our Long National Nightmare	65
Chapter 7	Mr. President	79
Chapter 8	1976	97
Chapter 9	Retirement	109
Selected Bibliography		121
Index		123

Preface

Gerald R. Ford, the Thirty-Eighth President of the United States, lived a life strikingly similar to the plot of a dime novel written during the time of his youth in the early Twentieth century, or of a Hollywood movie script of a generation later. The narrative is reasonably familiar: A young man born in the American heartland into modest, but not poor circumstances. He is shrewd and ambitious, although not brilliant in the academic sense. The youth perseveres through good times, and bad times, and embodies the virtues of hard work, self-discipline and proper conduct instilled by his parents. Ultimately, he succeeds, although this success is leavened with disappointments and setbacks. Gerald Ford's biography is, of course, much more complex than the Horatio Alger-novella sketched out above. Most observers would agree, however, that Gerald Ford did personify the All-American boy of his time and, to some extent, he made flesh the solid mid-western values of the burgher class he inherited from his family. Virtually everyone, political friend and foe alike, spoke well of Ford, honoring him for his character and his basic human decency.

The Ford Presidency defied such simple characterization. In fact, historical judgment concerning the Ford Administration has proved elusive and uncertain. The shifting historical consensus mirrors the pendulum effect of public opinion during the Administration itself. President Ford enjoyed a brief honeymoon period and a severe backlash following the Nixon pardon. The Ford team soldiered through the ups and downs of the Presidency, including a strong challenge from within his own Party, finally ending in the very close loss of November 1976. The historians began to evaluate the Ford Administration almost immediately and the early reviews were generally negative. Historians, political scientists and commentators criticized Ford's handling of the economy, his sometimes strained Congressional relations, and lingering questions about the Nixon pardon. Conservative critics attacked his embrace of the Kissinger-Nixon foreign policy, arguing that "détente" amounted to appeasement of the Soviet Union and the abandonment of former American friends to Communism.

These early criticisms of the Ford Administration may have been valid, but most were ahistorical in nature, and expressed the biases of the commentators more than the weaknesses of the Administration. Conversely, historians, political scientists and commentators of a more recent vintage are now ranking Ford much higher, as the fulsome tributes to the ex-President's memory upon his death on December 26, 2006 attest. Some historians now rank Gerald Ford in the "near great" category of all the Presidents. Such a lofty ranking of Ford might be overly generous, just as the early rankings of the former President were probably unduly harsh. Gerald Ford's historical legacy may still be in question. It is beyond question, however, that Ford brought honesty and integrity back into the White House at a time when the country needed those qualities and, in doing so, he restored a sense of calm to a troubled and anxious country. That is Gerald Ford's real legacy. He embodied the qualities and virtues of the American heartland and put these into practice in his public life. Gerald Ford was the All-American President.

This work will attempt to place President Gerald Ford in his proper position within the American pantheon. As the tumult and shouting of the 1970s fades into the increasingly distant past we can observe Ford without the ideological blinders that have obscured unbiased assessments of the man and his national stewardship. One of Ford's law professors at Yale summed him up as an honest and straightforward fellow of moderate ability, who worked hard and did well. This volume will concentrate on Ford as a solid Midwesterner who fairly radiated integrity and used his talent to earn high political office. In the office of the Presidency he sometimes disappointed his friends, as well as his foes. No one, however, questioned Ford's basic character. He lived up to his image as a classic Yankee success story, the All-American President.

ACKNOWLEDGMENTS

I would like to thank NOVA Science Publishers for extending me the contract to write this book. It has been a labor of love, and an education in itself. I would also like to thank Mary Grabar, Brian Elsesser, Bob Shea, Martha Patterson, Mark Abbott, Craig Piper, Paige Lewis and Catherine Platt for their interest, assistance and encouragement. I must also take the opportunity to thank my parents, James L. and Janet C. Birdnow for everything that they have sacrificed for me throughout these many years. Finally, I dedicate this volume to my darling daughter Caroline, the great joy of my life. Caroline, "Daddy's new book" is finished and dedicated to you!

FOREWORD

President of the United States of America is an official title sought by many and won by only a few individuals. Most American Presidents are of high merit and political acumen and reflected wisdom, leadership, and integrity. This series titled *First Men, America's Presidents* published by NOVA Science Publishers contains a book length biography of each President of the United States of America. Every book contains information on the President's early education, professional career, military service or political service prior to the presidency, interpretative discussion of both domestic and foreign policies during each presidency, and the conclusion of their political lives in public service. Every presidential biography in the NOVA series has been written by a professional historian or political scientist well versed in the field of presidential scholarship. The two major themes of this series are the character traits marking success in the presidency, and the changes in the office of the presidency through America's history. Character matters in all walks of life, but perhaps matters most within the character of the President of the United States.

The duties of the President of the United States are delegated through Article II of the Constitution of the United States of America, and from the successive laws passed by Congress over time. Each president takes the Oath of Affirmation:—"I do solemnly swear (or affirm) that I will faithfully execute the Office of the President of the United States, and will to the best of my Ability, preserve, protect and defend the Constitution of the United States." The president's duties and responsibilities under the Constitution are to serve as "Commander in Chief of the Army and Navy of the United States, and the Militia of the several States, when called into actual Service of the United

States." The president may invite the counsel and opinions of his various department heads upon any subject related to the execution of the duties of their offices, either in writing or orally as has become the custom within the president's Cabinet. The president "shall have the power to grant Reprieves and Pardons for Offenses against the United States, except in Cases of Impeachment." Every president has realized that each must administer through constitutional principles, as each was elected by the voting majority of the people to be their chief executive through the Electoral College. Each president of the United States "shall have Power, by and with the Advice and Consent of the Senate, to make Treaties, provided two thirds of the Senators present concur." As the president directs both the domestic and foreign activities of the government, he has the power to "nominate and by and with the Advice and Consent of the Senate ... appoint Ambassadors, other public Ministers and Consuls, Judges of the Supreme Court, and all other Officers of the United States, whose Appointments are not herein otherwise provided for, and which shall be established by law." The president also receives foreign ambassadors and officials on behalf of the American people. The president "shall have the Power to fill up all Vacancies that may happen during the Recess of the Senate, by granting Commissions which shall expire at the End of their next Session." The president under the Constitution shall give Congress a State of the Union address every year to acquaint them with his policy agenda and plans for the future. Usually in this address to Congress he recommends "to their Consideration such Measures as he shall judge necessary and expedient." Above all, the president of the United States "shall take Care that the Laws be faithfully executed, and shall Commission all the Officers of the United States." A strong role for the President had been envisioned by the Founding Fathers who rejected the obsolete Articles of Confederation and replaced the framework of government with the Constitution of the United States. Article II of the Constitution outlining the powers of the presidency provided that the office of the President would be held by one individual. It provided the President with enumerated powers including the power of the veto. And stipulated that the president's election would be above the control of the Congress to ensure the separation of powers and the system of checks and balances. It stipulated that the president, vice president, and all civil officers of the United States *must govern in the name of the American people* lest they "be removed from Office on Impeachment for, and Conviction of Treason, Bribery, or other high Crimes and Misdemeanors."

From Presidents George Washington through John Quincy Adams candidates for the presidency were selected in caucuses of senators and congressmen and then the state legislatures indirectly chose the president through the selection of Electors to the Electoral College. This system had worked for Washington, Adams, Jefferson, Madison and Monroe—they were statesmen who held wide appeal within Congress and the state legislatures and claimed to represent the people. But as demands for greater democracy in the election process were heard, the process was changed. In the outcome of the election of 1824, John Quincy Adams was chosen president by the Congressional House of Representatives under constitutional law after no candidate had received a majority of the electoral ballots in the Electoral College. Jackson, the candidate who had received the most popular votes was not chosen president and his supporters called for more direct popular participation and worked to introduce changes. Hence, the voting process was altered in the name of democracy. In the election of 1828 President Andrew Jackson triumphed after voting had been given directly to the people and removed from the state legislatures. Democracy further triumphed by the elimination of the congressional caucuses in naming presidential candidates and the holding of national political party conventions to name them instead, allowing greater voice and participation of the people. The institution of the party convention to nominate presidential candidates remains, although winners in various state primaries command party delegates to vote the choice of the people. The Presidency, molded by the character and designs of each president, oversees command, administration, diplomacy, ceremony, legislation, and public opinion. The modern strength of the Presidency is a reflection of the mighty power of the United States within a global world.

    The majority of America's presidents have served for one four-year term or less as some died in office. Four presidents served out part of their predecessor's term and won subsequent re-election in their own right: Theodore Roosevelt, Calvin Coolidge, Harry S. Truman, and Lyndon Baines Johnson. Only one president, Grover Cleveland, was elected to two discontinuous terms of office and thus was both the twenty-second and the twenty-fourth president of the United States. Several outstanding presidents have been elected to two four-year terms or more. They were: George Washington, Thomas Jefferson, James Madison, James Monroe, Andrew Jackson, Abraham Lincoln, Ulysses S. Grant, Grover Cleveland, William McKinley, Woodrow Wilson, Franklin D. Roosevelt, Dwight D. Eisenhower, Richard Nixon, Ronald Reagan, William Jefferson ("Bill") Clinton, and George W. Bush. Only one president, Franklin D. Roosevelt, was elected for a third and fourth term. Eight presidents have achieved their office as a result of being the vice-president of a preceding president who died in office or resigned: John Tyler, Millard Fillmore, Andrew Johnson, Chester Arthur, Theodore Roosevelt, Calvin Coolidge, Harry S. Truman, Lyndon Baines Johnson, and Gerald R. Ford. Additionally, John Adams, Thomas Jefferson, Martin Van Buren, Richard M. Nixon and George H.W. Bush also rose from the office of vice-president to president. Besides the vice-presidency as a stepping stone to the presidency, two thirds of the presidents elected had held congressional office earlier in their political careers such as Barack Obama, America's 44th President elected in 2008 who had served as a Senator from Illinois. Twenty presidents had served as Governors of states or territories before being elected. They were: Thomas Jefferson (Virginia), James Monroe (Virginia), Andrew Jackson (Florida), Martin Van Buren (New York), William Henry Harrison (Indiana), John Tyler (Virginia), James K. Polk (Tennessee), Andrew Johnson (Tennessee), Rutherford B. Hayes (Ohio), Grover Cleveland (New York), William McKinley (Ohio), Theodore Roosevelt (New York), William Howard Taft (The Philippines), Woodrow Wilson (New Jersey), Calvin Coolidge (Massachusetts), Franklin D. Roosevelt (New York), Jimmy Carter (Georgia), Ronald Reagan (California), William Jefferson Clinton (Arkansas), and George W. Bush (Texas). Some states with larger voting populations and hence more electoral votes have seen their native sons rise to the presidency of the United States. The American Presidents have come from both coasts, east and west, and from both the upper tier and the lower tier of states geographically, north and south. When elected, the president becomes the president of 'all the people', not just those of his political party. Since the president acts as America's commander in chief, the majority of the presidents of the United States have served in the U.S. military. George Washington, Andrew Jackson, William Henry Harrison, Zachary Taylor, Franklin Pierce, Ulysses S. Grant, Rutherford B. Hayes, James Garfield, Chester Arthur, Benjamin Harrison, and Dwight David Eisenhower served in the capacity of generals. James Monroe, John Tyler, Abraham Lincoln, William McKinley, Theodore Roosevelt, Harry Truman, John F. Kennedy, Lyndon Baines Johnson, Richard Nixon, Gerald R. Ford, Jimmy Carter, Ronald Reagan, George Herbert Walker Bush, and George W. Bush also served their country in military service at various ranks, and always with dedication. The youngest elected president was John F. Kennedy (1960) at forty-three. The youngest man to ever serve as president was Theodore Roosevelt who at forty-two assumed the office following William McKinley's assassination. The average

age for an elected president was fifty-four. The oldest elected president was Ronald Reagan at sixty-nine (1980) and seventy-three (1984).[1]

One of the major features of American constitutional development has been the growth of the presidency both in power and prestige as well as in new Cabinet positions, departments and agencies under the control of the president. The Federal government has grown mightily in comparison with the States' governments since the inception of the Constitution. Increases in presidential powers have been occasioned by wars, depressions, foreign relations, and the agenda of the presidents themselves. Henry F. Graff, Emeritus Professor at Columbia University, described the office of the president as "the most powerful office in the world" in *The Presidents*. The Executive Office of the President (EOP) was created during the administration of President Franklin D. Roosevelt upon passage by Congress of the Reorganization Act of 1939. The EOP originally included the White House Office (WHO), the Bureau of the Budget, the Office of Government Reports, the National Resources Planning Board, and the Liaison Office for Personnel Management. In addition, wrote Henry F. Graff, the 1939 Act provided that an "office for emergency management" may be formed "in the event of a national emergency, or threat of a national emergency."[2] Today the White House Office has become "the political as well as policy arm of the chief executive." The larger, all encompassing Executive Office of the President has expanded through time to include a myriad number of departments in addition to the first five listed above and the president is advised by nearly 60 active boards, committees and commissions. During and immediately after World War II the following additional departments within the purview of the EOP were organized: Committee for Congested Production Areas, 1943-1944, War Refugee Board, 1944-1945, Council of Economic Advisers, 1946-, National Security Council, 1947-, and National Security Resources Board, 1947-1953. During the Cold War, additions to the EOP were made adding the following departments: Telecommunications Adviser to the President, 1951-1953, Office of the Director for Mutual Security, 1951-1954, Office of Defense Mobilization, 1952-1958, President's Advisory Committee on Government Organization, 1953-1961, Operations Coordinating Board, 1953-1961, President's Board of Consultants on Foreign Intelligence Activities, 1956-1961, Office of Civil and Defense Mobilization, 1958-1962, and National

---

[1] David C. Whitney and Robin Vaughn Whitney, *The American Presidents,* Garden City, New York: Doubleday, 1993, pp. v-ix.

[2] Henry F. Graff, Editor, *The Presidents,* New York: Charles Scribner's Sons, Simon & Schuster Macmillan, 2nd edition, 1996, Appendix C pp. 743-745.

Aeronautics and Space Council, 1958-1993. By the Sixties, some of the earlier departments organized in the 1939 to 1960 decades were allowed to close, with newer agencies with a new focus and expanded technology taking their place. These newer agencies included: President's Foreign Intelligence Advisory Board, 1961-1977, Office of Emergency Planning, 1962-1969, Office of Science and Technology, 1962-1973, Office of Economic Opportunity, 1964-1975, Office of Emergency Preparedness, 1965-1973, National Council on Marine Resources and Engineering Development, 1966-1971, Council on Environmental Quality, 1969-, Council for Urban Affairs, 1969-1970, and Office of Intergovernmental Relations, 1969-1973. By the mid-Seventies, once again there was a general reorganization with some of the earlier departments and offices being swept away and replaced by newer agencies reflecting new presidential agendas. Many of the new agencies reflected the urgencies in domestic policies and included: the Domestic Council, 1970-1978, Office of Management and Budget, 1970-, Office of Telecommunications Policy, 1970-1977, Council on International Economic Policy, 1971-1977, Office of Consumer Affairs, 1971-1973, Special Action Office for Drug Abuse Prevention, 1971-1975, Federal Property Council, 1973-1977, Council on Economic Policy, 1973-1974, Energy Policy Office, 1973-1974, Council on Wage and Price Stability, 1974-1981, Energy Resource Council, 1974-1977, Office of Special Representative for Trade Negotiations, 1974-, Presidential Clemency Board, 1974-1975, Office of Science and Technology Policy, 1976-, Office of Administration, 1977-, and Domestic Policy Staff, 1978-1981. Many of the departments, councils and agencies organized as part of the Executive Office of the President by the late Seventies and early Eighties included: Office of Policy Development, 1981-, Office of the U.S. Trade Representative, 1981-, National Critical Materials Council, 1984-, Office of National Drug Control Policy, 1988-, National Economic Council, 1993-. By the 21st Century the EOP continued several effective agencies started earlier: Council of Economic Advisers 1946-, National Security Council 1947-, Council on Environmental Quality 1964-, Office of Management and Budget 1970-, Office of Science and Technology Policy 1976-, Office of Administration 1977-, Office of the U.S. Trade Representative 1981-, Office of Policy Development 1981-, and the Office of National Drug Control Policy 1988-. In addition to the White House Office of the president, the Office of the Vice President functions and is administered as part of the EOP.[3] At the turn of the millennium the department of Homeland

---

[3] Henry F. Graff, Editor, *The Presidents,* New York: Charles Scribner's Sons, Simon & Schuster

Security 2001- was established by presidential Executive Order and administered by the Executive Office of the President that continues to be evolutionary in response to new issues, demands, and events.

Capable presidents have responded to America's changing needs and responsibilities by retooling their administrations to meet new crises, opportunities, and challenges. This series *First Men, America's Presidents* published by NOVA explains the personal and public life of each President of the United States. Their qualities of character and leadership are aptly interpreted and offer strong role models for all citizens. Presidential successes are recorded for posterity, as are the pitfalls that should be guarded against in the future. This series also explains the domestic reasons and world backdrop for the expansion of the Executive Office of the President. The President of the United States is perhaps the most coveted position in the world and this series reveals the lives of all those successfully elected, how each performed as president, and how each is to be measured in history. The collective life stories of the presidents reveal the greatness that America represents in the world.

Dr. Barbara Bennett Peterson
First Men, America's Presidents NOVA Series Editor
Professor of History, Oregon State University (retired)
Emeritus Professor University of Hawaii
Former Adjunct Fellow East-West Center
Professor of History, California State University San Bernardino, Palm Desert (retired)

Macmillan, 3rd edition, 2002, Appendix C pp. 743-747.

Chapter 1

MAIN TRAVELED ROADS

Gerald R. Ford, Jr. The thirty-eighth President of the United States of America, the longest-lived American President, and one of the most unlikely, remains an elusive figure after his death. Ford's ascension to the Presidency from House Minority Leader, with a brief stop at Vice President took place over a nine-month period in 1973-74. This startlingly rapid ascent gave the American people little time to establish the identity of their new President. Ford had earned the respect, if not devotion, of his Congressional colleagues during a quarter century in the House of Representatives, but outside of Congress and his Western Michigan district Ford remained largely unknown. He set about creating a persona in the Presidency and became many things to different people. Late night television comedians found a rich vein of humor in Ford's supposed clumsiness and pratfalls, and this truly superb athlete became a national symbol for physical ungainliness. Political opponents considered him only marginally capable. While they admitted his good intentions, they questioned his ability. His own Party allies sometimes found him unimaginative and lacking in vision. Still, the American people seemed to find this new President reassuring. He exuded a sense of stability, steadiness of character, and the rock-solid values of an American who had grown to maturity through good times and bad, a college football star who had persevered through the Great Depression and World War II. The public sensed a man at ease with himself and the world, a man who approached his position with quiet confidence and carried out his duties with calm efficiency.

The real Gerald Ford story has proved to be much more complex than the simple myth people chose to believe. Gerald Rudolph Ford, Jr. was the product of a broken marriage, one punctuated by spousal abuse. His parents divorced at a time in which this was rare in America. The future President also faced strained family circumstances during the Great Depression and learned the value of hard work at an early age. He held many jobs including filling paint cans in the family business, washing dishes, and bussing tables in order to supplement his partial scholarship at the University of Michigan. Ford spoke of this in later years saying, "... I had plenty of adversity growing up. I just chose to accentuate the positive."[1]

The President also mentioned that few people were aware of the fact that he was not born Gerald R. Ford. The Ford story began in Omaha, Nebraska on July 14, 1913. Gerald R. Ford, who would become the thirty-eighth President of the United States, was born on this date as Leslie Lynch King, Jr. He was the son of Leslie Lynch King of Omaha, and Dorothy Ayer Gardner King of Harvard, Illinois. The future President's parents had married at Harvard on September 7, 1912 and had settled into a comfortable Victorian-style brownstone home on Woodlawn Avenue in Omaha. Leslie Lynch King, Jr. who would later be known to the world as President Gerald Ford was born into this home the following summer. Dorothy Gardner King was a nineteen-year-old college student when she met and soon married Leslie Lynch King, a man eight years her senior. King was a moderately prosperous Omaha businessman and the young couple seemed to enjoy a very bright future. Their future quickly faded as Mrs. King accused her husband of regular spousal battery. King, in fact, flew into a violent rage two weeks after the birth of the couple's son, brandished a bowie knife, and threatened to kill her and the baby. Dorothy King packed her belongings, took her son, and caught the first eastbound train out of Omaha traveling first to her sister's home in Oak Park, Illinois and eventually settling in with her parents at a new home in Grand Rapids, Michigan. A Nebraska state court granted Mrs. King a divorce on December 19, 1913.[2]

Grand Rapids, then the second largest city in Michigan provided opportunity and hope for many residents, circa 1913. The city had established itself as a furniture manufacturing center and presented a picture-postcard image of early twentieth century America, with an exceedingly clean and pleasant city rising out of the rolling farm country beyond. Grand Rapids, like many of the smaller cities of the time, possessed little in the way of cultural amenities and the city leaders tended toward a certain provinciality in their

---

[1] James Cannon, Time & Chance: Gerald Ford's Appointment With History: 1913-1974 (New York: HarperCollins, 1994) pp. 4-15.
[2] Gerald R. Ford, Genealogical Chart, found at Gerald R. Ford Presidential Library (GRFPL) Vertical File.

thinking. In historical hindsight one would be tempted to think of Grand Rapids as strongly resembling Sinclair Lewis' fictional "Zenith" and to dismiss the citizens as "Babbitts" of a sort. 1920s cultural stereotypes aside, though, many of the good citizens of Grand Rapids, from the established social elites, to the recently arrived Polish and Dutch immigrants, demonstrated most of the bedrock social virtues associated with the American Midwestern heartland. They were honest, self-disciplined, hardworking, and charitable to the less fortunate. The city was certainly not perfect, but Gerald Ford remembered his boyhood home fondly.

Dorothy Gardner King relocated to this somewhat idyllic city and began to rebuild her life in late 1913. At an Episcopalian church social in 1916 she made the acquaintance of a twenty-five year old paint and varnish salesman named Gerald Rudolf Ford. Although the "Ford" name was the gold standard in Michigan, Gerald could claim no kinship with the Detroit tycoon. He had dropped out of school after the tenth grade and gone to work, impressing bosses at various jobs with his work ethic and steadiness of character. Mr. Ford, in fact, seemed to embody the virtues of small-city America in person, and Dorothy King recognized these essential qualities immediately. Gerald Ford returned her interests and the couple married on February 1, 1917. The newly married couple settled into a comfortable home along with Mrs. Ford's son. The Fords began to refer to young Leslie as "Gerald R. Ford, Jr." although the future President didn't legally change his name until December of 1935. Moreover, Gerald Ford, Sr. never formally adopted his stepson because his wife suspected that adoption would work against her when she attempted to secure a child support judgment against her ex-husband, Leslie Lynch King. Mr. & Mrs. Ford told their son the truth about his parentage when he was thirteen years old.[3]

The future President of the United States spent his boyhood in a city, which mirrored the changing America of his time. Grand Rapids presented the Ford family a tableau of the gradually vanishing Norman Rockwell-style America, as the nation industrialized and urbanized during the Roaring 20s.[4] The Grand Rapids mercantile class practiced "boosterism," civic improvement, and honest politics as ways of establishing a favorable business climate, as well as naturally positive developments. The upper class in Grand Rapids tended toward philistinism in cultural and intellectual matters, as few considered the area a magnet for the fine arts. The city and its leading citizens,

---

[3] Douglas Brinkley, *Gerald R. Ford* (New York: Times Books, 2007) p.3.
[4] See Brinkley, *Gerald R. Ford*, pp.2-4, also see Cannon, *Time & Chance,* pp.4-12.

however, embodied the Middle American virtues of their time. They practiced thrift and frugality, honesty and self-discipline and supplemented these qualities with a basic decency in the form of charitable contributions and genuine concern for the less fortunate. Gerald R. Ford, Jr. imbibed these qualities during his childhood years.

During 1918-1927 young Gerald Ford attended primary school, spending a brief spell at East Grand Rapids Elementary School, but attending Madison Elementary School for most of those years.[5] "Jerry" Ford found plenty of time for extracurricular activities during his schoolboy days. He joined the local Boy Scout Troop 15 of Trinity Methodist Church, on his twelfth birthday in July of 1925. He took scouting very seriously, and, showing the diligence that would mark his public career, he attained the rank of Eagle Scout, the highest position in the organization in 1927. Gerald Ford is the only American President to have been an Eagle Scout.

Gerald Ford graduated to South Grand Rapids High School, which he attended from 1927-1931. Ford blossomed during his High School years, becoming, in many ways a Michigan version of the All-American boy. Ford participated in the Student Council, the Glee Club, the Latin Club, and the High School YMCA, among other volunteer groups. He proved himself to be a good, but not exceptional student, earning membership in the National Honor Society and the Varsity Letter Club. One of the high points of Ford's secondary schooling years came during his senior year when he won a contest to determine the most popular boy in his class. The prize for winning this contest was an-all-expenses-paid trip to Washington D. C. in the summer of 1931. Ford never forgot the sense of awe he felt as he watched the House of Representatives in action. Ford resolved, in his mind, at that point that he would return to Washington someday as a member of Congress. When he did return, he stayed for twenty-nine years! Ford's newfound interest in public affairs did not, however, define his persona. Competitive team sports were the lifeblood of Jerry Ford's High School years.

The myth of Gerald Ford as a clumsy man, prone to tripping over his own feet has embedded itself in the consciousness of two American generations, thanks in large part to the NBC television program *Saturday Night Live*. This durable fable masks the truth that Gerald Ford may have been the most athletically gifted man ever to hold the American Presidency. An inner ear difficulty, developed in mid-life, adversely affected Ford's balance, but he

---

[5] Gerald R. Ford Timeline, found at GRFPL, Box 88.

emerged as a superb athlete in high school.[6] He excelled in track and basketball, while also boxing and playing baseball. Later, in adulthood, Ford became an accomplished ballroom dancer. Football, however, became Gerald Ford's signature sport.

Jerry Ford starred on the gridiron for the Grand Rapids South High School varsity football squad during his final two years of school. He played center and earned all-city honors for his outstanding contributions to his team during his junior year in the autumn of 1929. He bettered this sterling performance during his senior year, earning all-state recognition in the autumn of 1930, playing on a state championship squad. Ford earned a name for himself through his prowess on the gridiron and this helped him to attend college, which he financed partly through campus jobs that he otherwise might not have secured. Ford's athletic experiences certainly touched him deeply and he often used sporting metaphors during his public life. Moreover, competitive sports ingrained in the young man an understanding of the importance of teamwork, determination, and preparation as prerequisites for success. They also instilled in him a sense of fair play and adherence to established rules that would stand him in good stead as he climbed the ladder in politics.

During Ford's schooling years his family life rounded out, as well. His mother gave birth to a son, Thomas Gardner Ford on July 15, 1918.[7] Interestingly, the first two of the Ford boys shared consecutive birthdays. The family grew again on June 3, 1924 with the birth of a third boy, Richard Addison Ford, and the family welcomed their final member, James Francis Ford, to the world on August 11, 1927.[8] The family, by most accounts lived happily and in modest comfort. Gerald Ford, Sr. worked hard in the paint and varnish business to provide for his brood, in a middle class section of the city. His son later remembered the father attending to his affairs and steadily building a business. Ford also remembered that his father set few rules but insisted that his sons should work hard, tell the truth, and come to dinner on time. Mr. & Mrs. Ford spent their spare time in charitable and philanthropic activities; one of which they were particularly proud was establishing a recreation center in a poorer section of Grand Rapids.[9]

In the late summer of 1929 Gerald Ford, Sr. seemed to be living a classic Middle American dream. He and a small group of investors founded the Ford Paint & Varnish Company, and he moved the family into a comfortable new

---

6 Paul Johnson, A History of the American People, (New York: HarperCollins, 1997) p. 906.
7 Gerald R. Ford, Genealogical Chart, found at GRFPL, Vertical File.
8 Ibid.
9 Cannon, Time & Chance, p. 15.

home on Lake Avenue, located in the fashionable east side of Grand Rapids. This idyllic existence ended with chilling suddenness in October of 1929. The Stock Market crash that year nearly strangled the infant business in its cradle and completely emptied the family savings account. The Ford family left their new home for cheaper accommodations and settled in grimly to attempt to outlast the Great Depression.

During the hard times of the early 1930s the Ford family struggled like millions of others. The future President of the United States said later that no one went to bed hungry, although they didn't eat very well.[10] Jerry Ford, himself, did what he could to help out by mowing lawns, cleaning and refilling paint cans at the family business, washing dishes at a restaurant, and grilling hamburgers at a stand across the street from his school. He actually met his birth father while working at the stand one summer afternoon in 1930. According to Ford's autobiography, he was working at the hamburger stand when a well-dressed man and his female companion pulled up in a new Lincoln Continental, and parked at the curb. The couple looked intently at him for a few minutes, the man approached the stand, and asked Jerry his name. Jerry supplied the information and the man identified himself as "Leslie Lynch King, your father."[11] Young Jerry secured a lunch break from his boss and went out to eat a sandwich with his theretofore unknown father and stepmother. Mr. King said that he and his wife were living in Wyoming, and had interests in sheep and cattle ranching, along with oil and natural gas. They happened to be in Michigan because they had bought the new car directly from the Ford plant in Dearborn and were now heading home. They asked Jerry if he cared to come and live in Wyoming with them and he rejected the offer. At length, the lunch hour drew to a close and the Kings prepared to set on about their homeward journey. Leslie Lynch King reached into his pocket and gave his son twenty dollars, a fairly considerable sum in 1930. He wished his son well and headed westward to Wyoming. At home that night Ford told his parents about the meeting and handed the twenty dollars over to his mother. He later recalled that he cried that night after going to bed.[12]

All in all, the Ford family mirrored the middle class American experience of their age, enjoying the prosperous years of the 1920s and doggedly enduring the hardships of the Great Depression. Gerald Ford grew to maturity in this environment. He imbibed many of the virtues and moral lessons

---

10 Gerald R. Ford, A Time To Heal: The Autobiography of Gerald R. Ford (New York: Harper & Row, 1979) pp. 40-45. See Also, Brinkley, Gerald R. Ford, p. 4.
11 Ibid. pp. 46-48.
12 Cannon, Time & Chance, p. 16.

imparted by his family and the larger society. The future President exhibited leadership skills in school, on the athletic fields, and in social organizations. He applied himself and worked hard at all endeavors, proved to be a capable student with a quick mind, although he showed little intellectual pretense. Ford earned the good opinion of the adults of his community, and developed a reputation as a young man of character and potential. In the late summer of 1931 Gerald Ford took the next step along his personal journey. The All-American boy graduated from secondary school and went off to college. The University of Michigan and gridiron fame awaited him, just around the corner.

Chapter 2

HAIL TO THE VICTORS

Jerry Ford's good mind, solid character, and general ability showed often and, having been one of the best students in his secondary school class, he certainly proved worthy of a university education at a time when this was still an exception to the rule in America. The tales of his gridiron exploits traveled widely and Ford visited Harvard, Northwestern, and Michigan State Universities, along with other colleges. While Ford impressed the coaches and admissions officials at these institutions the problem facing him was financial in nature. The Great Depression had hit America in late 1929 and was fully underway by the time Ford graduated from Grand Rapids South High in June of 1931. The economic downturn hit Grand Rapids and the Ford family business particularly hard. The paint and varnish business appealed to few, as customers worried more about keeping their homes, than painting them. Ford knew he could count on little help from his family, and his goal seemed out of reach.[1]

At this critical juncture a number of University of Michigan alumni led by Arthur Krause, the Grand Rapids South High principal, went to work on Ford's behalf, albeit without his knowledge. Krause telephoned the Michigan Athletic Department and spoke to the legendary athletic director Fielding "Hurry-Up" Yost and to Harry Kipke, the head football coach, explaining the plight of the All-State center. Kipke, whose job involved following and monitoring potential football stars, knew all about Gerald Ford and agreed to make a recruiting visit to the Ford home in the spring of 1931. Kipke took Ford to Ann Arbor, arranged a small scholarship, (the University did not offer

---

[1] Cannon, *Time & Chance*, p.16.

full athletic scholarships at the time) and helped Ford secure a job at the University hospital waiting on tables to earn his living expenses. Impressed by Coach Kipke's open manner and his kind assistance, Ford eagerly accepted the opportunity to attend Michigan and to play football for the Wolverines.

The only difficulty, in this otherwise promising scenario, was the fact that Ford did not possess the $100.00 tuition fee required by the university in 1931.[2] The Ford family, barely scraping by during the early days of the Great Depression, could do nothing. Arthur Krause, knowing that Ford was a National Honor Society student, as well as a football star, again interceded on his former student's behalf. He established an annual college scholarship and inaugurated the award by offering it to Jerry Ford, and announcing that the scholarship would go to a student who combined academics, athletics and citizenship in a manner bringing credit to his alma mater. Although the scholarship helped out, strained financial circumstances continued to plague Ford throughout his college years. He found himself fairly deeply in debt during his senior year and took on extra jobs in order to finish his education. A long letter to his natural father in Wyoming requesting financial assistance went unanswered.[3]

Jerry Ford arrived on the University of Michigan campus in September of 1931. He majored in economics and proved himself to be a good, though not outstanding student. He did well in history, literature, and government courses and earned acceptable marks in Latin and French. Ford found the going a bit tougher in calculus, chemistry, and physics but he studied hard and generally acquitted himself well. He finished with a solid "B" average, quite an honor in those pre-grade inflation days.

Barred from immediately playing football by the freshman exclusion rule in place at the time, Ford chose to immerse himself in other extracurricular activities during his early college years. He joined Delta Kappa Epsilon fraternity during his freshman year at the urging of Dave Conklin, a former football opponent who now attended Michigan and would be a teammate of Ford's on the Wolverine team in the future. Ford later became the DKE representative to the Inter-fraternity Council, and a member of the student council, as well. He genuinely enjoyed the masculine "bonhomie" of the fraternity life, and this undoubtedly influenced his ideas concerning the

---

2 Ibid p.17.
3 Brinkley, Gerald R. Ford, pp. 6-7, also see Ford, A Time To Heal, pp. 51-53.

manner in which the U.S. House of Representatives should operate a generation later.[4]

Ford played the role of Big-Man-On-Campus to the hilt during his Ann Arbor years. At the close of his junior year in 1934 Ford gained membership in the "Sphinx" club, an unofficial University honor society for the undergraduate class. He followed up this distinction by garnering induction in the elite "Michigamua" society, an even more exclusive club composed of outstanding university seniors. Ford made many lifelong friends at Michigan and broadened his cultural horizons at the same time. He visited the homes of friends and teammates in Detroit, and while in the city he attended performances of the Symphony Orchestra and the Detroit Opera, although he didn't care for either art form, especially opera. He joined fraternity buddies and other friends on weekend trips to Chicago, where he attended sporting events, live theater, and the occasional burlesque show. These experiences opened young Ford's eyes to a world theretofore unknown, but also deepened his appreciation for his roots in Grand Rapids, the small city in the American heartland, and his home.

Academics and extracurricular activities, however important they may have been in rounding Ford's character, played a secondary role to his athletic responsibilities. In fact, Gerald Ford's most significant contributions at Ann Arbor came, naturally, on the football field. By this time, Ford had matured to his adult height of six feet and three/quarter inches tall and he scaled between 185-190 pounds.[5] At the University he found himself playing at center on offense, and at linebacker on defense in the still customary two-way player system. The Michigan Wolverines fight song is entitled, *"Hail To The Victors"* and the team certainly lived up to the title of their anthem during Ford's first two years on the squad. In fact, Ford and the Wolverines captured consecutive national championships in 1932-33. Ford found, however, that the competition at the college level was much tougher than he had expected and certainly more difficult than anything he had ever encountered. Due to the freshman exclusionary rule Ford and his fellow football recruits served as the scout team in September of 1931, practicing with the varsity and helping to prepare the team for each weekly game. Jerry Ford found this somewhat humdrum routine to be a valuable learning experience in the sense that it introduced him to the different styles of football he would encounter in the Big

---

[4] Lewis Gould, *The Modern American Presidency"* (Lawrence, Kansas: University of Kansas Press, 2003) p. 173.
[5] Gerald R. Ford Timeline, found at GRFPL, Box 88.

Ten Conference. He zealously devoted himself to training and impressed the coaching staff with his dedication. After the spring practices in 1932 he was named the Wolverines most improved player.[6]

During the national championship seasons of 1932 and 1933 Ford spent most of his energies cheering his teammates on from the bench. Chuck Bernard, the team's starting center, was a consensus All-America choice and Jerry Ford served as a second stringer. Ford insisted in later years that he learned more about football while watching from the bench than actually playing, however, he did admit that the new experience of backing up a more seasoned player was somewhat humbling. Still, Ford emerged as the consummate team player, and no one demeaned his contributions to the two time national champions. In Ford's senior season of 1934 he made the starting squad and emerged as a true team leader. He served as an assistant team captain, started every game, and earned honors as a first team All-Big Ten selection at the center position. At the conclusion of the season the team chose Ford as their Most Valuable Player.[7] The only sour note in Ford's senior year was the inescapable fact that the Michigan team, depleted by the graduation of many star players, won only one game that 1934 season.

Ford's Michigan squad lost their final game of the 1934 season to Northwestern. The following week, the Northwestern coaching staff extended Ford an invitation to play in the annual East-West Shrine Game in San Francisco, on New Year's Day, 1935. This game, a charity benefit, generally served as a showcase for college stars, and also attracted many sportswriters and professional scouts. Ford considered his selection to the team to be a great honor and he later found out that his strong play in the season finale at Northwestern had impressed the opposition's coaches so much that they chose him for the East team.[8] Ford later remembered that the professional scouts and coaches largely ignored him on the train trip to San Francisco. They spent time interviewing and evaluating the better-known players. During the early part of the game, however, George Anderson of Colgate, the East team's starting center fell heavily to the turf and broke his leg. Ford subbed in immediately, played the rest of the game, and remembered it as one of his finest gridiron performances. His impressive work earned him an invitation to play in the College All-Star Game the following summer. In what turned out to be Jerry

---

6 Gerald R. Ford Biographical Information, found at GRFPL, Vertical File.
7 Cannon, Time & Chance, pp. 19-20, also see Brinkley, Gerald R. Ford, p. 6.
8 Cannon, Time & Chance, p. 10.

Ford's last competitive football game he and his All-Star teammates lost to the Chicago Bears 5-0.[9]

After Ford's impressive showing in the East-West Shrine and College All-Star contests he became a hot property and the professional scouts who had overlooked him now showed interest in the former Wolverine star. The Green Bay Packers submitted Ford a contract offer for $110.00 per game, for a fourteen-week season. The Detroit Lions bettered the Green Bay package by offering $200.00 per game, also for fourteen weeks.[10] Ford thanked the teams for their interest, but politely declined their offers. If he had accepted the Detroit contract offer he would have played on an NFL championship team in 1935, as the Lions won the league title that season, defeating the New York Giants in the championship game by a score of 26-7. Ford admitted in later years that refusing the Green Bay and Detroit offers was a tough decision. He had decided to attend law school at the earliest possible moment, but there may have been other factors in play, as well. Professional athletes rarely commanded stratospheric salaries in 1935, and pro football, especially, seemed to appeal to a lower middle class clientele. It was a rough and tumble sport, played by sturdy men, most of working class origin. Long NFL careers were a rarity and most pro football veterans finished their tenures after numerous injuries rendered them expendable. Many college-educated gentlemen, including Heisman Trophy winners like Jay Berwanger and others, eschewed professional football and pursued more traditional careers. Gerald Ford had already made up his mind to run for office and devote himself to public service, so he declined offers to continue playing his best sport.

While Jerry Ford may have decided to attend law school, he had apparently neglected some of the necessary preliminary work in deciding where to go to law school and, more importantly, how he proposed to finance this new undertaking. He decided to pursue his studies at the highly prestigious University of Michigan School of Law and approached his mentor, Coach Harry Kipke, about the possibility of financing his studies by taking a job as an assistant coach of the football team. Coach Kipke gave Ford the bad news that he couldn't pay for an assistant coach due to the still persisting Great Depression. The continuing economic downturn ensured that Gerald Ford's career path would take him somewhere other than law school in the autumn of 1935.

---

9 Brinkley, Gerald R. Ford, p.7.
10 Gerald R. Ford Timeline, found at GRFPL, Box 88.

So, as Jerry Ford approached his college graduation he faced an uncertain future. During the grim times of the early-to-mid-1930s many formerly prosperous college-educated men had been reduced to selling pencils and apples on street corners. By 1935 conditions had improved somewhat, but unemployment remained alarmingly high and Ford's own prospects seemed somewhat limited, as a Bachelor of Arts degree in economics did not open many doors. In April, Coach Kipke called Ford and told him that Yale University was looking for an assistant football coach. He added that Yale's head coach, "Ducky" Pond happened to be in Ann Arbor at that time and asked Ford to join them for a luncheon meeting.[11] The three men met and discussed this possible opportunity. Ford found, to his surprise, that Coach Pond knew him by reputation. Ivan Williamson, a Yale assistant coach, had been the captain of the Michigan team during Ford's sophomore season and strongly endorsed his former teammate as a new hire. Coach Kipke gave Ford a glowing vote of confidence during the luncheon meeting and Coach Pond, suitably impressed, invited the erstwhile All-Big Ten center to New Haven for a short visit and formal job interview.

The weekend visit went splendidly well. Jerry Ford liked the Yale campus and the New England countryside, and his football experience, poise, and seriousness of purpose impressed his prospective employers. Coach Pond, speaking for the Yale Administration, offered Ford a job as an assistant offensive line coach, at $2,400 per year. The offer came, however, with an unexpected wrinkle. The Yale Administration also insisted that Ford coach boxing and his pugilistic experience was very limited. He approached this point honestly, but stated that he would learn everything necessary to tackle the extra duties. Once again, Ford's earnest manner, his honesty, and his calm but serious demeanor carried the day. The Yale Administration guaranteed Coach Pond's job offer, spelling out the fact that Ford would coach football in the fall and spring and boxing in the winter. He would have a three month summer vacation, and would earn the agreed upon compensation of $2,400 per year. Ford accepted the position immediately, explaining in later years that the coaching position paid him fairly well at a time that the nation was still battling the Great Depression. Furthermore, he believed that this connection might somehow open the door to admission at Yale Law School.

Jerry Ford graduated from the University of Michigan in June of 1935. He skipped the University Commencement ceremony and went back to Grand Rapids to refill paint cans in the family business for the summer. He worked in

---

[11] Cannon, *Time & Chance*, p. 20.

the family business during the day and spent late afternoons and evenings at the Grand Rapids YMCA taking boxing lessons, training, sparring and learning as much about the sport as possible.[12] Ford, a naturally gifted athlete, proved a quick study in the ring, easily grasping the fundamentals of the sport and becoming a competent boxer by the end of the summer. He mastered the foundation of the sweet science and coached capably at Yale for five years.

During the summer of 1935 Ford also tied up some loose ends of a personal nature. He sat down with his parents one evening and informed them that he wanted to legally change his name to Gerald R. Ford, Jr. Everyone who knew him had called him Jerry Ford for many years, but his legal name was still Leslie Lynch King, Jr. Ford stated that he wanted to show his respect and devotion to the man who had raised him as his own son.[13] Shortly after his twenty-second birthday in July of 1935, Ford filed a petition for a change of name with the Michigan authorities. Gerald and Dorothy Ford, always proud of their son, openly wept at his expression of love and reverence. The following day, with no fanfare, Ford filed a formal application for a name change, in the Probate Court of Kent County, Michigan. The court confirmed the request on December 3, 1935.

The new assistant football coach arrived at Yale in the late summer of 1935. Yale, then as now, ranked as one of the most prestigious private universities in the United States. Most of the Yale student body were graduates of the top New England prep schools like Choate, Andover, Exeter and Deerfield. Generally, Yale men possessed strong intellect, but also good family connections, and sometimes, substantial family fortunes. Social position certainly mattered at Yale and the incoming freshman class of a given year would include the names of many of the most prominent American families.

An intellectual atmosphere permeated the Yale campus and the academic departments were universally strong. Yale challenged the students in every imaginable way, and football was one of many extracurricular activities stressed by the institution as a character-building pastime. The Yale football program also produced some superb players. Offensive end Larry Kelly won the Heisman Trophy awarded to the nation's best college football player, in 1936. His teammate Clifton Frank, a halfback, won the award the following year, 1937. When Jerry Ford stepped onto the Yale practice field in September of 1935 he had never coached football at any level. Ford found, however, that

---

12 Brinkley, Gerald R. Ford, p. 6.
13 Gerald R. Ford Timeline, found at GRFPL, Box 88.

having played on two national championship teams and having earned All-Big Ten honors conferred a certain legitimacy on himself that he otherwise might have lacked. He had a certain natural ability and easily settled into his new position. Ford adopted a calm and pedagogical approach to coaching by stressing the fundamentals of blocking and tackling.[14] He taught his players proper technique, and shared many trade secrets that he had picked up during his Michigan years.

Ford became a master motivator, seeking to improve his players and drawing the maximum effort out of each individual. William Proxmire, later a U.S. Senator from Wisconsin, played at Yale and flourished under Ford's tutelage. Proxmire, who also excelled at boxing under Ford's direction, remembered his coach as "... very conscientious and diligent. A good mind, a first rate mind."[15] Robert Taft, Jr. who would later represent Ohio in the U.S. Senate remarked that Ford wasn't a hothead who yelled and screamed to make his points. Instead, "Coach Ford was very calm and spoke to your intelligence. He taught the basics, like blocking and tackling, by telling and showing you how."[16]

Coach Ford liked his job and remembered his Yale years fondly. He learned many lessons that would serve him well later in public life, especially in the U.S. Congress. He remembered later that he learned the importance of taking "orders" in the sense of accepting direction and fitting into a hierarchical structure designed by the boss. He realized that each assistant had to carry out certain specific duties if the team were to have a chance of success. Ford also understood his role as a formal representative of Yale University. He was expected to uphold the honor and dignity of the institution in the community, at alumni gatherings, on other Ivy League campuses during the season, and on recruiting trips while visiting the family homes of prospective players.

While Ford attended to his duties and built his reputation as a coach he continued to harbor aspirations to attend Yale Law School, and saved money toward that end. Frugal by nature, Ford rented a small and inexpensive apartment. He opened a savings account at a New Haven bank, shunned luxuries and high living, and saved money with law school as his ultimate goal.[17] The mere fact that Ford had chosen Yale, as his preferred destination guaranteed nothing. The institution ranked among the most selective of

---

14 Cannon, Time & Chance, p. 21.
15 Ibid. pp. 21-22.
16 Gerald R. Ford Genealogical Chart, found at GRFPL, Vertical File.
17 Cannon, Time & Chance, p. 23, see also Brinkley, Gerald R. Ford, p.7.

American legal colleges. Ford apparently never considered the possibility that his application might be rejected, or that he could encounter academic difficulties in law school. Ford knew that he had been a solid student at Michigan, earning a "B" average and garnering a fair share of honors in the process. He had failed to earn *cum laude* status at Michigan, but enjoyed the respect of professors and classmates as a bright and hardworking student. He considered himself a shoo-in for law school admission.

In the spring of 1936 Coach Ford informed his superiors in the Yale Athletic Department of his desire to attend law school. The bosses flatly told Ford that the prospect seemed out of the question. They praised Ford's coaching performance and informed him that his salary would be raised to $3,000 a year. Malcolm Farmer, the Yale Athletic director, said that the university expected coaches to work full-time, thus Ford could not attend law school. At the same time, Yale Law School itself rebuffed the aspiring counselor. An Admissions Officer brushed off Ford's inquiry by pointing out that the law school rejected three-fourths of all applicants, further pointing out that nearly 80% of the incoming Class of 1939 were Phi Beta Kappa Honor Society members. Ford, stung somewhat by this letdown, temporarily put aside his law school plans, but continued to prepare for the future.[18]

Ford's immediate plans concerned the upcoming summer of 1936. His Yale contract gave him the summers off, and paid him during the summer months. Ford could have enjoyed a paid vacation, indulged in pleasure, or loafed if he had so chosen. Gerald Ford, however, showed the work ethic instilled in him by his parents and his Midwestern upbringing, decided to work during the summer, as a matter of course. He briefly considered returning to Grand Rapids to pass the summer working for his father, but he had lost interest in the paint and varnish business.[19] One of Ford's fellow assistant coaches had spent two summers as an apprentice forest ranger at Yellowstone National Park, and mentioned this as a possible opportunity. Ford admitted that such a position appealed to him in a way that refilling paint and turpentine cans did not. He used his family connections to arrange an interview for a job, and secured the appointment. He bought himself a car, and, after stopping in Michigan to see his parents, made the long drive west.

After a short and uncomfortably tense side-trip to visit his father, Leslie King, and his stepmother in Riverton, Wyoming, Ford proceeded to the National Park site. The forest service assigned Ford to the Canyon station and

---

[18] Cannon, *Time & Chance*, p. 23.
[19] Ibid. pp. 23-24.

he spent three months as an apprentice forest ranger tending to generally mundane tasks such as assisting tourists and directing traffic along with more exciting duties like managing wildlife and fighting fires. Ford's nice-guy demeanor won him many friends and the summer left him permanently enchanted with the natural beauty of the Big Sky country. In Congress, Ford became a stout supporter of the National Park system and an advocate for the preservation of the American West.[20]

When his idyllic summer ended in August of 1936 Ford began his return drive to New Haven and another season of coaching. He stopped off in Grand Rapids to spend a few more days with his parents and to regale them with stories of his exciting summer. He also mentioned his visit to his father's ranch in Wyoming and the fact that the man seemed to be weathering the hard times very well.[21] The summer of 1936 served as a tonic to Jerry Ford. He arrived in New Haven at the end of August tanned, trim, and fully enthusiastic about his second year of coaching. He also resolved to find a way into Yale Law School.

Ford resumed his coaching activities on the campus in September of 1936 and continued his now familiar routine. During the year his mother filed a legal action against his natural father for back child support. Attorneys battled over the case for months and finally Leslie Lynch King agreed to pay his ex-wife $4,000. After a deduction for court costs and attorney fees Mrs. Ford received a certified check for $2,393 and forwarded this to her son at New Haven. Jerry Ford promptly returned the check to his mother, saying that she deserved it after the pain and heartache of her broken marriage. Ford never saw or heard from Leslie Lynch King, his father, ever again.

While coaching and working his way through this domestic conundrum Ford decided to employ an alternate plan to gain admission to Yale Law School. He enrolled at the University of Michigan Law School for the summer term in 1937.[22] He hoped that he could prove his mettle by taking classes and earning good marks, thus showing enough potential to impress the Yale admissions office. Ford earned "B" grades in both of his classes and found that he enjoyed the academic rigors of law school. When Ford retuned to New Haven for the 1937 football season he once again applied for admission to Yale Law School, this time reinforcing his package with good grades from a highly respected law school in their summer program. Still, Yale proved a tough nut to crack, and two Deans rejected Ford's application. In a personal

---

[20] Ford, *A Time To Heal*, p. 55.
[21] Ibid. p. 56, see also Cannon, *Time & Chance*, pp. 25-26.
[22] Cannon, *Time & Chance*, pp. 23-24.

interview, however, Ford impressed the influential Professor Myres McDougal, who recommended that the school should admit the earnest young football coach.[23] McDougal expressed some concern at Ford's supposed lack of solid academic preparation, but considered him mature, poised, and serious. This character analysis mirrored the general consensus opinion of Jerry Ford as someone who fairly radiated the virtues and values of his time. Professor McDougal's words apparently carried some weight and Yale Law School admitted Gerald Ford into the institution on a trial basis. He received permission from the Athletic Department to attend law school part time and the school allowed him to enroll in two classes during the spring term in 1938.

The young football coach/student applied himself to his studies and, once again, earned "B" grades in his courses. He also continued to coach boxing and spring football, executing all of his duties and responsibilities capably. Ford noted in later years that he worked harder in the spring of 1938 than he ever had before, and he found himself thoroughly exhausted at the end of the spring term. He again found the experience of legal studies to be intellectually stimulating and he convinced himself that he could successfully navigate the treacherous waters of Yale Law School while continuing as a popular and promising football coach.[24]

In the fall of 1938 the Athletic Department raised Ford's pay to $3,600 per year and increased his responsibilities by naming him the director of recruiting as well as head boxing coach, junior varsity football coach and head assistant for the offensive line on the full football squad. Regardless of the increased responsibility and workload Ford still managed to successfully negotiate two more legal classes during the fall term in 1938. He neglected to tell the coaching staff that he was attending law school, and similarly withheld the information that he was still working fulltime as a football coach from the law faculty. In December of 1938 Ford informed his Athletic Director supervisor, Malcolm Farmer that he would continue to study law while coaching, if the university would consent to that type of arrangement, but that he would resign to attend law school otherwise. The Athletic Department valued Jerry Ford's coaching ability and admired his work ethic. They rescinded the pay increase that they were prepared to offer him for the following year, but allowed him to stay on as an assistant football and boxing coach while he attempted to work his way through Yale Law School.[25] Jerry Ford did not realize at this moment

---

[23] Brinkley, *Gerald R. Ford*, p. 8.
[24] Ford Family Documents and Genealogy chart, found at GRPFL, Vertical File.
[25] Ibid.

that his life, like the lives of millions of Americans, would change immeasurably in the next few years.

Chapter 3

AMERICA FIRST?

The Yale Law School, Class of '41 was, arguably, the most talented cohort ever to grace that august institution. The class included Gerald Ford, a future President, Potter Stewart and Byron R. White, each a future Supreme Court Justice, Sargent Shriver, the first director of the Peace Corps, Cyrus Vance who would serve as Secretary of State, Pete Domenici, who represented New Mexico in the U.S. Senate, and the distinguished novelist and historian Walter Lord.[1] The football coach and future President acquitted himself very well at Yale. He ranked in the top third of his class and earned a solid "B" average. One of Ford's professors, Eugene Rostow, a future Undersecretary of State, recalled Ford as, "A very solid, straightforward, decent sort of bird of moderate ability. He worked hard, did reasonably well."[2] Once again Ford's nice-guy persona, earnest manner and basic decency impressed many people as fundamental to his essential character.

In fact, Ford's law school interlude offers a useful vantage point from which to view his general mode of operation and accomplishment. Gerald Ford, by most accounts, dazzled no one at Yale. His professors and classmates liked and respected him. He earned a reputation as a hardworking and earnest student who pushed himself hard and usually accomplished what he had set out to do. Ford's achievements, however, were seen as the fruits of hard work and careful planning, not the result of innate brilliance or talent. Ford refused to be outworked or out hustled, although he could, at times, be out maneuvered. The future U.S. Representative and President was offering a

---

[1] Cannon, Time And Chance, p. 29.
[2] Brinkley, Gerald R. Ford, p. 7.

preview of his public life. He set goals, worked doggedly hard to achieve them and usually accomplished most of what he had outlined as a program to his friends and confidants. Often Ford left his opponents (and sometimes his friends) scratching their heads as to how this seemingly amiable and guileless Michigander ended up besting them. Beginning with his days at Yale Law School people tended to underestimate Gerald Ford, choosing to overlook his character and his increasingly shrewd nature.

While studying law and coaching football Gerald Ford also experienced the first truly serious love affair of his life, during the years 1938-41.[3] A female friend from Ann Arbor sent Ford a note in the autumn of 1938 and suggested that he contact Phyllis Brown, a student at the Connecticut College For Women, at New London, about fifty miles from the Yale campus. Ford's acquaintance had attended prep school with Miss Brown, found her charming and attractive, and urged Ford to contact her. Two weeks later Gerald Ford called Phyllis Brown, introduced himself and asked her out for dinner. She accepted his invitation and he drove to New London to meet her. The couple developed a mutual attraction, which quickly bloomed into a full-blown romance. Phyllis Brown, the daughter of a department store owner from Lewiston, Maine was, indeed, beautiful, stylish and vivacious.[4] She presented quite a contrast to Gerald Ford, the serious and purposeful football coach and aspiring law student. Phyllis Brown noted this contrast in later years when she pointed out that Ford, even at that time, was an earnest and hardworking young man. She stated that all the time Ford had spent working in jobs and other projects had interfered in the other aspects of his life. He had never had time for a serious girlfriend. She also stated that she, herself, was a fun loving party girl who wanted to experience all that life had to offer. Despite, or perhaps because of their differences, their romance took off.

Ford considered Phyllis Brown his first love and their courtship commenced with a whirlwind of activity. They played golf and tennis; they swam in the summer and skied in the winter. Phyllis taught Ford to play bridge, while he schooled her in the finer points of poker. They read novels aloud, took joy in everyday affairs and generally delighted in each other's company. The couple ratcheted up their romance in early 1939 when Phyllis, quite by accident, met a photographer/graphic artist who arranged an interview for her at the John Roberts Powers agency in New York. The agency offered

---

[3] Cannon, *Time And Chance*, p. 27. Also see, Brinkley, *Gerald R. Ford*, p.7, Ford *A Time To Heal*, pp. 56-57.
[4] Cannon, *Time And Chance*, p. 27.

Miss Brown a contract, which she promptly accepted. She withdrew from college and moved to New York City.[5] In order to continue the romance Jerry Ford commuted to New York regularly. He and Phyllis made the Big Apple their personal playground, visiting the museums and parks, restaurants, the opera and theaters, and also going to the ballpark. The couple celebrated Phyllis twenty-first birthday by dancing at the Rainbow Room at Rockefeller Center, while the lights of Manhattan lit the darkness around them. The couple reveled in this magical existence.[6]

Phyllis Brown's modeling career flourished amidst the bright lights of Manhattan, and she made a name for herself in the field. She secured a lucrative continuing engagement as the cover girl for *Cosmopolitan* magazine. In the winter of 1940, *Look* magazine invited her to take a boyfriend to Vermont for a ski weekend/photo shoot and she chose Jerry Ford. The photo shoot appeared in seventeen pages of the March 12, 1940 issue of the magazine. The couple dressed in ski togs and posed on the slopes of Stowe, Vermont. They also appeared snuggling together during a sleigh ride, and warming themselves by a fire in the ski lodge. The couple would reprise this interlude for a patriotic *Cosmopolitan* photo shoot in early 1942.[7]

The young lovers spent early summers together at the Ford family home in Grand Rapids and then passed August together at the Brown family estate in Maine.[8] Jerry Ford impressed the Brown family as he impressed most people. He seemed to be a polite and earnest young man, largely free from pretense and affectation. The respective families in Michigan and New England assumed, as a matter of course, that Jerry Ford and Phyllis Brown would marry, settle down and raise a family. Ultimately, though, the love affair cooled down and eventually fizzled. Ford had volunteered to assist the Wendell Willkie presidential effort in 1940 and he enlisted Phyllis in the campaign, as well. Ford reached a crossroads in his still-young life at this moment. He saw the finish line in law school shortly ahead and knew that his football coaching days, happy though they had been, were now behind him.[9] The Willkie campaign energized Ford, and steered him in the direction of public life himself. He politely declined job offers at New York and Philadelphia law firms and quietly, but firmly, decided to return to Grand

---

[5] Ibid. p. 28.
[6] Ford, *A Time To Heal*, pp. 56-57. Also see Cannon, *Time And Chance*, p. 29, and Brinkley, *Gerald R. Ford*, pp. 7-8.
[7] Brinkley, *Gerald R. Ford*, pp. 7-8.
[8] Cannon, *Time & Chance*, pp. 29.
[9] Gerald R. Ford, Genealogical and Biographical Information, found at GRFPL, Vertical File.

Rapids and open a law office. Ford would remark in later years that he was a Midwesterner at heart, and that Grand Rapids was home. He also admitted that it would be easier to run for public office in Grand Rapids, where his father had built a business and raised his family, rather than having to contend with the anonymity factor of a very large metropolis like New York or Philadelphia.[10]

Ford agonized over this decision. He knew that Phyllis Brown would not give up her promising and exciting modeling career and easily adapt to the role of a Michigan housewife. They both realized that their idyll was coming to an end. Ford told Phyllis that he was going to move back to Michigan to practice law. She suspected that the Willkie campaign had awakened a public service interest in her gentleman friend and that he intended to run for office at the earliest opportunity. She agreed that his place was back home in Michigan, but she also knew that she could never successfully master the role of a congressional spouse. Jerry Ford and Phyllis Brown realized that their romance closed at this moment. They parted on good terms, treasured the memories, and went their separate ways.

The ambitious young attorney remembered the break-up of his romance as a difficult period and one that left him downcast for a time. He later determined that the differences in personality and nature between himself and Phyllis would have rendered a happy and stable marriage an unlikely prospect.[11] The two saw each other a few times in later years, but their courtship ended in 1941. Gerald Ford, like millions of other American males opened a new chapter in his life that fateful year.

While Gerald Ford coached and attended law school at Yale he gradually developed a nascent political ideology. His views were rough and somewhat unclear, and he would reverse himself on a number of big issues over the years. Nevertheless, this man who freely admitted having few ideological convictions began to develop a political philosophy during his Yale Law years. Ford's philosophical bedrock foundations developed from his family and upbringing. Ford's youth and teenage years seemed to exemplify the solid burgher values of his time. His upbringing and family life, while not the mythical Norman Rockwell-like existence that some have surmised, announced "American Heartland" proudly and freely. Jerry Ford, the Eagle Scout, the scholar athlete, the hardworking and honest young man who grew

---

[10] Cannon, *Time And Chance*, pp. 29-30.
[11] For Western Michigan's Republican nature and Ford's own GOP inclinations see Ford, *A Time To Heal*, pp. 62-64.

into a pillar of the community, fairly radiated All-American values. He professed the virtues of hard work, thrift, probity, prudence and a deep (if somewhat understated) love of country. Jerry Ford imbibed these ideals from his public civics lessons, but he also lived these ideals in his personal and public lives.

Ford also inherited a party identity from his family. Western Michigan, then a GOP stronghold, attracted most of the business class in Grand Rapids including Gerald R. Ford, Sr. The Ford family patriarch, universally respected and well-liked in the city, identified himself as a Republican man. This GOP partisanship translated, in fact, into a mild and non-ideological party identity and certainly did not intrude upon friendships and business relationships with those who identified themselves as Democrats. Gerald Ford, Sr. took an active role in the local Republican organization, eventually becoming a county chairman. He adopted most of the traditional GOP positions, disapproved of the New Deal, and found the statist thrust of Roosevelt's second term vaguely ominous. He remained, however, respectful of the President and the institution, and maintained friendly relations with all, regardless of their politics. Ford passed these qualities along to his stepson, who saw his stepfather as a personal role model.[12]

Jerry Ford gravitated naturally toward the Republican Party. He found a political home in the Party of Lincoln and Theodore Roosevelt, which, in turn, welcomed a person such as him, a man of character and reputation. Ford, as a result of class and family origins, found the center-right Republicanism of his father to be a safe harbor in the increasingly turbulent days of the late 1930s and early 1940s.

The singular event defining those times was, of course, the outbreak of the Second World War, with the German invasion of Poland on September 1, 1939. The stark reality of war once again shocked the world, and in America there existed a strong current of conviction that the nation should take the necessary steps to stay out of the European conflict. President Roosevelt announced American neutrality in a nationwide radio address on September 3, 1939, and this statement of nonaligned status reflected the thinking of a significant segment of the American population. American public opinion began to shift, however, in the spring of 1940. The speed and apparent ease of the German conquest of Denmark, Norway, Belgium, The Netherlands, and France alarmed the American public and this sense of impending danger reached flashpoint as the Germans launched an all-out aerial assault on Britain

---

[12] William DeGregorio, *The Complete Book of U.S. Presidents,* (New York, 1984) pp. 458-459.

during the late summer. Live radio broadcasts of the German Air Forces pounding London from the air added to the mounting sense of urgency and crisis.[13]

There still existed in America, however, a substantial and vocal opposition to the war. The most outspoken anti-interventionist group organized during the prewar period was known as the "America First Committee," an isolationist group formed in September of 1940. The group was formed and funded by Robert E. Wood of Chicago and contained among its members such distinguished personages as Colonel Robert McCormick, the publisher of the *Chicago Tribune*, aviation hero Charles Lindbergh, and financier Joseph P. Kennedy, among others. The committee resolved to support a United States effort to defend itself and the Western Hemisphere from foreign invasion, but not to send expeditionary forces overseas to fight. This sentiment resonated strongly in the traditionally isolationist Midwest, and influential members of Congress defended the America First Committee's position.[14]

Gerald Ford joined the America First Committee while he studied at Yale Law School. He followed the lead of classmates like Kingman Brewster, Potter Stewart, and Sargent Shriver and advocated full neutrality in the war then raging in Europe. In Jerry Ford's case the adoption of a neutralist position concerning the war was fairly natural, and certainly heartfelt. Isolationist thinking had deep roots in Michigan and the upper Midwest. A considerable segment of the population in the heartland had opposed American involvement in the First World War, and the difficulties the nation encountered in making peace, demobilizing, and securing repayment of the loans the financial sector had made to our former allies seemed to vindicate the non-interventionist position. Furthermore, the non-interventionists deeply distrusted British financial and commercial power. The emergence of the strange and portentous ideologies of Bolshevism, Nazism, and Fascism in Europe after 1918 led many Americans, Gerald Ford among them, to conclude that America was correct in steering clear of the European calamity.

Ford gradually moved away from his neutralist position and became a committed internationalist, although his journey was halting and tenuous. He took his first steps in the direction of an internationalist position when he attended a Wendell Willkie rally in New York in March of 1940. He liked what he heard and decided to work for the Willkie campaign. Willkie

---

[13] Clarence B. Carson, *A Basic History of the United States*, (American Textbook Committee, Wadley, Alabama, 1986) p. 108.
[14] Brinkley, *Gerald R. Ford*, p. 7.

supported direct American assistance to Britain and a more activist foreign policy, which separated him from his Republican rivals, Governor Thomas Dewey of New York, Senator Robert Taft of Ohio, and the man who would become Ford's political mentor, Senator Arthur Vandenberg of Michigan. Ford brought his girlfriend, Phyllis Brown, in to work for the Willkie campaign, as well. They performed mostly routine tasks, but Ford managed to parlay his work into a seat at the Republican convention at Philadelphia in the summer of 1940 as a Willkie delegate.[15]

Ford finally moved to the internationalist position after Pearl Harbor, World War II, and his own military service. He saw American world leadership as a great force for peace, freedom and a more just international order, mirroring the views of thousands of war veterans like himself. In fact, Ford ultimately followed the path set by his mentor, Senator Vandenberg, in moving from a generally isolationist point of view, to one that became unabashedly internationalist in nature.

Gerald Ford took his first steps on the road that would one day lead to the White House in the summer of 1941. He had finished law school and made good his decision to move back home and practice law in Grand Rapids. In New York he had met up with an old fraternity brother named Phil Buchen who had graduated from the University of Michigan Law School and was working as a legal clerk in Manhattan. Buchen intended to stay and practice in Gotham, but Ford urged him to join in a partnership and to practice "at home" in Grand Rapids. Ford employed all of his persuasive powers on his old fraternity buddy, pointing out that they could be their own bosses in Grand Rapids, and that the Ford name, being well known in the city, would open some doors. Buchen, initially cool to the idea, changed his mind and agreed to set up a partnership in Grand Rapids. The two aspiring counselors sat for and passed the Michigan Bar Exam in the summer of 1941. Each man then contributed one thousand dollars to a general business fund, and they formed Grand Rapids newest law firm, Ford & Buchen, with an office (Suite 321) in the city's tallest skyscraper, the Michigan Trust Building, located in the bustling downtown area.

Jerry Ford would later remark that Ford & Buchen landed a client on their first day in business. A man came to the office and hired the firm to perform a title search. The fee amounted to five dollars! Clients did not easily materialize for the new law partnership, but Ford & Buchen managed to stay a step or two

---

[15] Cannon, *Time And Chance*, p. 30.

ahead of the debt collectors.[16] They generated just enough business to pay their expenses, as they began the slow and laborious task of building a profitable law practice.

While Ford and Phil Buchen labored mightily to ensure the professional success of their partnership, they also found other ways to stay busy during their homecoming year. Jerry Ford was, by his own admission, a "compulsive joiner" and he found numerous outlets for his energies. He taught a course in business law at the University of Grand Rapids and he took on a part-time role as an assistant football coach at the University, as well. On occasion, Jerry Ford, an eligible bachelor, would take a young woman out to the movies or to dinner, but he spent most of his time working and trying to establish himself in his profession. Ford remained the earnest and hardworking young man he had always seemed to be and his good reputation followed him. It would be a mistake, however, to consider Ford to have been an ordinary plodder who simply trudged along the career path. Ford's genial, nice-guy persona masked a deep and driving ambition. Ford had a facility for meeting and making the acquaintances of people who could help him out in many ways. He was not above using these friendships to advance his prospects. Similarly, Ford's propensity for joining clubs, civic groups, and other organizations proved helpful in getting to know the most important people in his community on a personal basis. Many of these people would become Ford's core group of campaign volunteers and loyal supporters when he stood for office in the future.

While Ford went about the business of building his law practice he did not neglect his political interests. All Ford biographers agree that he harbored political ambitions and he made his first forays into the harsh world of practical politics in 1941. Ford possessed the requisite good name and reputation necessary for a political future, and his law practice, though growing, did not yet make crushing demands on his time. Ford found his political sea legs in the summer of 1941, in the form of opposition to the regular Republican organization in Western Michigan.[17] Jerry Ford's first political enemy was a man named Frank McKay, a politician of the rough-and-tumble sort who exercised influence as the Republican "Boss" of the western side of Michigan. McKay, himself, eschewed public office, but wielded political power through his control of every patronage position in every level

---

[16] Ibid. p. 32.
[17] Gerald R. Ford Timeline, found at GRFPL, Vertical File.

of government in Michigan's Fifth Congressional District.[18] McKay also controlled most of the state public works contracts, primarily for the highways and state parks. McKay had earned a fortune in banking, real estate, and insurance and often claimed that he was a businessman, not a politician. Still, everyone knew that McKay was the boss of the Western Michigan Republican machine, and the man who could make or break a political candidacy in the state.

Jerry Ford had first crossed paths with Frank McKay in the summer of 1940. Ford, home on a summer break after finishing the spring, 1940 term at Yale Law School, called on Boss McKay at his downtown Grand Rapids office, intending to volunteer to work for Republican candidates. The GOP boss kept Ford waiting hours for an appointment and essentially ignored his offers to campaign for party candidates. Ford took this brush-off to heart as a grave insult and looked forward to the day when he would turn the tables on the McKay machine.

After returning to Grand Rapids in 1941 Jerry Ford and a number of associates, including his father who served as the chairman of the Kent County Republican Committee, Phil Buchen, Ford's law partner, and assorted reformers and good government types cobbled together a very loose alliance dedicated to the goal of toppling Boss Frank McKay and his machine. The possibility of a greenhorn coalition besting the seasoned professionals of the McKay machine seemed a longshot, at best. The quixotic effort ground to a temporary halt in early 1942 as many of the conspirators went off to war. Those who stayed behind began to refer themselves as "The Home Front" and continued to prepare for the future.[19]

On the fateful afternoon of December 7, 1941 Gerald Ford ignored the Biblical admonition to rest on Sunday and went to his law office to prepare for a court appearance the following Tuesday. He worked until the late afternoon, left the office, and heard the shocking news of the Japanese aerial attack on Pearl Harbor on his car radio as he drove home. Over dinner that evening Ford told his parents that he would volunteer for service and join the navy, and he submitted his application for a commission in the United States Naval Reserve on February 23, 1942. He took his oath and earned a commission as an Ensign on April 20, 1942.[20]

---

[18] Brinkley, *Gerald R. Ford*, p. 8.
[19] Ford, *A Time To Heal*, pp. 63-64. Also see Cannon, *Time And Chance*, pp. 44-45, Brinkley, *Gerald R. Ford*, pp. 8-12.
[20] Gerald R. Ford Timeline, found at GRFPL, Vertical File.

The Navy sent Ford to Officer Indoctrination School at the Naval Academy for one month in the spring of 1942, and he was promoted to Lieutenant, Junior Grade in that capacity. The military had thoroughly checked Ford's background and, aware of his gridiron stardom and coaching credentials, they decided that he would serve most ably as a physical training instructor. Ford preferred a sea assignment and was disappointed when he received orders to report to a Navy preflight physical training unit based at Chapel Hill, North Carolina. He joined his unit as a "physical fitness specialist" and served under the command of Colonel Gene Tunney, the legendary former heavyweight boxing champion. Lieutenant j.g. Ford impressed upon the pilot recruits the importance of physical conditioning, and he certainly looked every bit the athlete during the war years. Ford's official War Department personnel file listed him at slightly less than six feet-one inches tall and weighing 192 pounds.[21] His waist measured a slender thirty-one inches and he retained the broad chest and shoulders of a former All-Big Ten offensive lineman. Ford adapted easily to military life, enjoying the masculine camaraderie of the officer corps, and he earned outstanding fitness reports from his superior officers.

While many officers would have considered themselves fortunate to have landed stateside in a comfortable preflight training school billet, Gerald Ford chafed at what he considered insignificant duty. He yearned to get into the fight then raging around the world and twice applied for transfers to sea duty, only to be refused each time. On the third go-around Ford's request for transfer was approved. He was promoted to Lieutenant and ordered to report to Norfolk, Virginia for gunnery training. After completing this training Ford was assigned to the new light aircraft carrier the USS *Monterey*. This interesting warship sported a 622-foot flightdeck positioned on top of a standard cruiser hull. The ship could carry forty-five aircraft and was outfitted with forty anti-aircraft guns.[22]

Lieutenant Ford sailed aboard the USS *Monterey* from the Philadelphia Navy Yard in the spring of 1943. The new carrier underwent local testing operations in the Caribbean Sea, passed through the Panama Canal, and proceeded to San Diego to load her complement of fighter planes, dive bombers, and torpedo bombers. The new ship then sailed westward at top speed to join Admiral William F. "Bull" Halsey's Third Fleet in the Central

---

[21] Ibid.
[22] Ford, *A Time To Heal* p. 58. Also see Brinkley, *Gerald R. Ford,* p. 9, Cannon, *Time And Chance,* p. 34.

Pacific.[23] During the underway period Ford served as the ship's athletic officer and he earned the thanks of the crew for rigging a basketball court on the hangar deck. He took greater personal interest, however, in his duties as a gunnery officer and devoted himself to mastering his responsibilities with his characteristic dedication.

In November of 1943 the *Monterey* joined the larger carrier the USS *Enterprise*, and a small contingent of escort ships to assist in the island hopping campaign throughout the West Central Pacific. The campaign unfolded with the *Monterey* using her planes and anti-aircraft guns blasting the Japanese defenses at Makin Island in the Gilberts chain, and then moving south-southwest to strike at the Japanese base at New Ireland on Christmas Day, 1943. Lieutenant Ford directed a battery of 40mm anti-aircraft guns on the fantail deck firing at Japanese attackers. During this combat the *Monterey* was credited with sinking a Japanese cruiser and a destroyer and in Ford's words, "…it was as much action as I'd ever hoped to see."[24]

Ford transferred to a collateral position as assistant navigational officer at the end of 1943. He made friends among the ship's senior officers including Captain Lester Hundt, his commanding officer, who was an ardent football fan. Ford learned seamanship from Commander "Pappy" Atwood, a former merchant sea captain who had been conscripted into the uniformed service for the duration of the war. Atwood, a vastly experienced seadog, taught Ford the basics of navigation and maneuvering a large ship. Ford apparently learned his lessons well and earned a spot on the bridge, as Officer of the Deck during General Quarters, which gave him a central role during combat. The young attorney-turned-gunnery officer relished his new role. He had yearned for sea and combat duty and thrived on the action.

In 1944 the *Monterey* supported the amphibious invasions of Kwajalein and Eniwetok islands and, the following month, went into action against the Japanese at Truk, the heavily fortified island stronghold in the Carolines. The ship supported actions at Palau and Hollandia, Saipan, Tarawa, Guam and against the Japanese surface navy near the Marianas islands. In the Philippine Sea the *Monterey* bombers sank a Japanese cruiser. The ship sustained damage during the kamikaze attacks, while her bombers struck the Japanese defenses on Formosa. In slightly over one year in action the ship and crew earned thirteen battle stars.

---

[23] Ford, A Time To Heal, p. 58.
[24] Ibid.

Lieutenant Jerry Ford soon emerged as one of the ship's most popular officers. He developed a reputation as an officer who genuinely cared about the welfare of his men, and looked out for them. Ford's noted calm demeanor seemed to reassure many of the young draftees. As Ford biographer Mark Cannon has noted, "To the ranks of sailors, Ford was something of a Mr. Roberts."[25] He remained the self-possessed, solid, instructional type he had been as a college football coach, the sort who led by example, rather than exhortation. Ford's fitness reports documented his outstanding service and his overall character. The reports stated that Ford was a natural leader, universally respected by his men, and personally popular among his colleagues. Captain Stuart Ingersoll, the new skipper of the *Monterey,* personally recommended Ford for a promotion to the rank of Lieutenant Commander.

Ford's sea duty concluded with the near sinking of the *Monterey* in a terrifying storm approximately six hundred miles off the Luzon coast in the East China Sea. Typhoon Cobra hit Halsey's fleet in December of 1944. This violent disturbance produced one hundred knot winds and nearly eighty-foot seas. The raging water simply capsized three American destroyers and killed over eight hundred sailors and marines, including six men from the *Monterey*.[26] Jerry Ford narrowly avoided sliding overboard off of the rolling hangar deck of the carrier and then performed heroically by fighting numerous fires, and helping to keep the crippled vessel afloat through the storm. The *Monterey* sustained such heavy damage that the Navy officials declared the ship unfit for further service, and ordered her back to home port at Bremerton, Washington for extensive repairs.

Lieutenant Ford immediately applied for reassignment to another carrier in the Western Pacific as the war now thundered toward a climax. The Navy, though, had other ideas and ordered Ford back to the Great Lakes training station, near Chicago, to await new orders. He separated, in an emotional fashion, from the *Monterey* and his fellow officers and shipmates on Christmas Eve, 1944. Ford took two weeks of leave, visited his parents in Michigan, and flew to New York to see his old acquaintances from the New Haven days, including his former girlfriend, Phyllis Brown. He met Phyllis, who had married and was expecting a baby, for drinks at a hotel bar. Ford was no home-wrecker and he described their meeting as cordial, but nothing more.

---

[25] Cannon, Time And Chance, p. 35.
[26] Brinkley, Gerald R. Ford, p. 11.

The former couple finally realized that their romance was over, as too much water had flowed under the bridge during their years apart.[27]

When Ford's leave ended he reported to his new duty station at the Naval Training Command attached to the Great Lakes facility in Glenview, Illinois. He returned to his former role, training young officers for action at sea or in the air and was promoted to Lieutenant Commander in April of 1945. Ford longed to return to sea duty and actively lobbied for a reassignment to the carrier USS *Coral Sea*, or any other available ship, as the military prepared to deliver the knockout blow against Japan. Ford capably executed his duties, while hoping for orders to return to sea, until Japan surrendered on August 14, 1945.

World War II changed Gerald Ford, just as it changed each of the sixteen million Americans who served in the armed forces. They fought to defend the nation and to defeat her enemies. Over three hundred thousand had been killed and countless numbers wounded. The survivors had demonstrated and witnessed heroism, courage, self-sacrifice and the entire range of human emotions. They experienced foreign cultures and new lands and most of the participants understood the world much differently as a result of their service. Lieutenant Gerald R. Ford emerged from the war physically unscathed, but ideologically changed. He freely admitted to having been an isolationist before the war, taking to heart George Washington's admonition against entangling alliances. He claimed, however, that his wartime experiences had given him a new perspective and that he returned to civilian life an "ardent internationalist."[28] He pledged himself to support a strong peacetime military force and to work to assist our allies, and the unfortunate neutral states caught in the maelstrom of war, in the arduous task rebuilding their shattered nations.

Lieutenant Commander Gerald R. Ford officially separated from the United States Navy in February of 1946. He sensed that he would soon reach a crossroads in his life. The ex-officer was nearly thirty-three years old, he had to re-establish himself in his civilian career, and many crucial decisions lay just ahead. As Jerry Ford, still young, but now aging, returned to Grand Rapids in 1946 he prepared to embark on the next adventure of his remarkable life.

---

[27] Cannon, Time And Chance, p. 38.
[28] Ford, A Time To Heal, p. 61.

Chapter 4

THE DISTINGUISHED GENTLEMAN FROM MICHIGAN

The future President of the United States returned home to Grand Rapids in the winter of 1946. His most pressing problem was the same difficulty confronting millions of returning veterans, namely the need to restart his temporarily shelved civilian career. He knew that the old law firm of "Ford & Buchen" no longer existed. His old law partner, Phil Buchen, disabled by polio from childhood, was exempted from the military *levee*. During the war Buchen had joined "Butterfield, Keeney, and Amberg" the most prestigious law firm in Grand Rapids, as a junior partner. When Ford returned home he and Buchen discussed the possibility of re-establishing their old firm, but eventually decided against the idea. Julius Amberg, a senior partner at Butterfield, Keeney, & Amberg offered a possible solution to Ford's dilemma. Amberg invited Ford to join the firm as a junior associate and told him that, while the firm could not offer Ford a partnership immediately, they planned to do so in the near future. Amberg, a classmate of the legendary jurist Felix Frankfurter at Harvard Law School, promised to make Gerald Ford a first rate attorney. He proved to be as good as his word, taking Ford under his wing, and serving as a mentor and a sounding board during Ford's years with the firm.

Ford took on many complex cases for his new firm and put his interest in business and economics to work by handling many thorny cases involving trusts, estates, wills and securities transactions. While he learned the law by practicing he also built a good reputation as a promising figure in the community. In his autobiography, Jerry Ford remembered himself as a "joiner" and he took on active roles in the American Legion and the Veterans of Foreign Wars, speaking often of the need for affordable housing for veterans.[1] He also worked with the Red Cross, the Grand Rapids public schools, and, at the invitation of fellow veterans, he joined the Michigan chapter of the National Association for the Advancement of Colored Peoples. Ford's civic-mindedness and steady character undoubtedly served as his motivation for these endeavors, but he certainly understood the value that membership in such organizations provided to an aspiring politician. Gerald Ford intended to run for public office as soon as practicable and, in joining many civic groups he garnered needed name recognition and developed a loyal following of friends and supporters who would serve him well in the future.

In fact, a close look at Gerald Ford's life to 1946 showed that he had a remarkable ability to develop friendships and to impress people who could later prove useful to him. In every venture Ford met and cultivated individuals whose friendships distinctly helped him in life. He attracted attention with his steady character, his likeable demeanor, and his serious, but affable nature. Ford did not shun the attention that he earned. He proved to be a sharp fellow on the make, who set his sights high and capitalized on the good impression he made on friends, acquaintances and professional associates. He would demonstrate this clearly in his first foray into public life in 1948.

During his stint in the military Jerry Ford kept in contact with the "good government" reform group he had helped to found in Grand Rapids. Ford referred to this group as the "Home Front," tying in his struggles with the politics-as-usual crowd in Michigan with the national struggle against imperial Japan. When Ford returned home he decided to re-ignite the largely moribund reform movement with the ultimate goal of toppling the Western Michigan Republican machine and Boss Frank McKay. Ford's key allies in this plan turned out to be his old friend Willard Ver Muelen, a Grand Rapids dentist, Julius Amberg, his legal mentor, and his father Gerald R. Ford, Sr. who won election as Kent County Republican Chairman in 1945.[2] This small band of co-conspirators moved stealthily and methodically toward achieving their goal in the immediate postwar years.

During these years Gerald Ford also fleshed out a generally center-right political philosophy, which would guide him throughout his entire public career. Ford staked out a classic orthodox Republican position on fiscal matters, claiming that the nation could not solve complex problems simply by throwing money at them. He tended toward moderation on social issues, although his record on civil rights would prove tenuous and somewhat uneven.

---

[1] Ford, *A Time To Heal*, p. 62.
[2] Gerald R. Ford Timeline, found at GRFPL, Vertical File.

On foreign policy Ford placed himself firmly in the Internationalist camp, largely as a result of his wartime experiences.[3] He fully supported the Democratic President Harry Truman on the question of foreign aid and retaining a standing military establishment during peacetime. In these matters Ford followed the lead of Senator Arthur Vandenberg, also of Michigan, whom he thought of as a political mentor. Vandenberg abandoned his earlier isolationist views and supported many Democratic foreign policy initiatives, beginning with the Truman Doctrine in early 1947. Vandenberg broke with those in his own Party, notably Senator Robert Taft of Ohio, who reflexively opposed Truman's internationalism.[4] Ford, who had known Vandenberg personally as a family acquaintance, firmly positioned himself as an internationalist, albeit a conservative internationalist, in foreign policy.

While Ford continued his development into a center-right public man the "Home Front" faction operated quietly and carefully in pursuit of their long range goal of toppling the powerful McKay machine. They operated secretly for fear that the McKay forces would learn of their existence and take defensive action. The McKay machine had actually suffered a number of reverses in the immediate postwar period, having to contend with a series of state investigations concerning highway contracts in Western Michigan, but the organization remained in place and no one thought that a small group of upstarts could depose Boss Frank McKay and his henchmen. Ford, his father, and their associates calmly decided to target U.S. Representative Bartel (Barney) Jonkman for defeat in the Republican Party primary election on September 1, 1948.[5] Jonkman, a four-term Congressman, supported an isolationist foreign policy and was widely regarded as a tool of the McKay organization. Western Michigan, specifically the 5th Congressional District, qualified as safe Republican territory, so winning the GOP nomination in the primary was tantamount to winning a general election.

The reform faction silently set about recruiting a candidate to run against Jonkman, but found that no one seemed to welcome the prospect of carrying the fight to the McKay machine. After refusals from a number of potential candidates the reformers convinced Jerry Ford run for the seat.[6] Ford recounted in his memoirs that each time he asked someone to consider running against Jonkman they declined, but urged him to make the race himself. He

---

[3] Brinkley, *Gerald R. Ford*, p. 13.
[4] Cannon, *Time And Chance*, p. 44. Also see Brinkley, *Gerald R. Ford*, pp. 16-17, Ford, *A Time To Heal*, pp. 61-67.
[5] Cannon, *Time And Chance*, pp. 44-45. Also see Brinkley, *Gerald R. Ford*, pp. 10-11.

finally began to consider the possibility and conceded that the idea made perfect sense. Ford agreed that he would run against Barney Jonkman in the 1948 Republican primary election, in the Michigan 5th Congressional District.

Since the Home Front faction considered caution an imperative in their movement Ford waited until June 14, 1948, a mere three months before the primary election, to announce his challenge to Jonkman. The McKay forces had heard the buzz about a possible test of their man but shrugged the possibility off as nothing more than a minor annoyance. Ford, however, soon proved his mettle and the seriousness of his challenge by actively campaigning throughout the entire congressional district. Julius Amberg, Ford's boss at Butterfield, Keeney & Amberg, gave him a virtual leave of absence to campaign during the summer and served as an unofficial consultant on legal matters. Ford framed his challenge to Jonkman as a foreign policy debate between an internationalist and an isolationist, but the election actually played out as an assault on an old fashioned political machine. The attack on the McKay organization was by no means a single incident of this type. Many of the older city political machines were beginning to crumble in the face of a changing mid-twentieth century sociopolitical landscape. The 1948 Republican primary in Michigan's 5th Congressional District served as a public referendum on Boss Frank McKay.

On primary election day September 14, 1948 Gerald R. Ford, Jr. easily defeated incumbent Congressman Bartel Jonkman by a final tally of 23,636 to 14,314. Ford rolled up impressive margins winning nearly every township and ward in the district. He ran well in rural and urban areas and proved that he was not a fluke of nature, but a promising young politician who would be a force in the future. Ford knew that winning the Republican nomination in Western Michigan virtually guaranteed victory in the general election. He refused, however, to take anything for granted and campaigned hard in advance of the November 2, 1948 general election contest. Ford stumped the district, worked the rope line at county fairs, picnics, and parades and he campaigned for the entire Republican ticket from Presidential candidate Thomas Dewey on down to local hopefuls. He even delayed his marriage to Betty Bloomer Warren until October 15, 1948 in order to devote more time to campaigning. After a one-day honeymoon he got back on the campaign trail again. On the first Tuesday of November in 1948 Gerald R. Ford won the first of thirteen elections to the U.S. Congress, garnering 60.5% of the vote.[7]

---

[6] Ford, *A Time To Heal*, pp. 63-64.
[7] Brinkley, *Gerald R. Ford*, p. 13.

Gerald Ford, the former All-Big Ten center from Michigan was now U.S. Representative Gerald R. Ford, the distinguished gentleman from Michigan.

Freshman Congressman Gerald R. Ford, Jr. was also a newly married man. In Ford's own words, "Betty just lit me up. She touched me in a way that no other woman ever could."[8] Elizabeth Anne (Betty) Bloomer obviously set Gerald Ford back on his heels and changed his life for the better in 1947. Jerry Ford threw himself into his professional and public life upon his return from military service in early 1946. He had little time for social frivolities and had not been involved in a serious romance since his liaison with Phyllis Brown before the war. His friends, and more particularly, his family, began to worry about his future. Ford recalled in later years that his mother chided him in the spring of 1947 about the fact that he hadn't "settled down" into marriage and family life, that he was getting older, and that he still lived in his parents' home.[9] His mother and father seemed convinced that their son still harbored deep feelings for Phyllis Brown, the great love of his early life.

In fact, Jerry Ford had given a great deal of thought to his future. He wanted a wife and a family, but could not find the right woman. He mentioned to friends that he found few local women interested in dating a thirty-four year old bachelor. Frank and Peggy Neuman, a married couple of Ford's acquaintance, suggested a friend of theirs named Betty Warren, a vivacious twenty-nine year old going through a divorce, as a possibility. Ford knew of Betty only slightly, but remembered her as a very attractive woman. He decided to take a chance on Betty Warren and the end result became a storied marriage.

Elizabeth Anne Bloomer Warren Ford was born on April 8, 1918 in Chicago, Illinois to William and Hortense Neahr Bloomer. The family, including Betty and two older brothers, resided in Chicago until 1920 when her father, William Bloomer, an industrial machinery salesman, moved his brood to Grand Rapids, Michigan. Betty attended Grand Rapids Central High School and graduated in 1936. During her school years Betty took dancing lessons, specializing in ballet, tap, and modern jazz. She decided to pursue a career as a professional dancer after spending her High School summers as a dance coach and instructor.[10] Betty Bloomer took her next steps toward a career as a professional hoofer by attending the Bennington College of Dance in Bennington, Vermont. There she met Martha Graham, the renowned

---

[8] Ibid.

[9] Ford, *A Time To Heal*, p. 62.

[10] Betty Ford Genealogical Documents, found at GRFPL, Vertical File.

choreographer and accepted Ms. Graham's offer to join the highly exclusive Martha Graham Dance Company.

Betty moved to New York in 1939 to continue her dance studies with the Martha Graham troupe. She perfected her technique and gained much needed refinement while performing in public forums. In order to finance her living expenses Betty worked part-time as a model at the John Roberts Powers agency. Betty continued to dance with the Graham auxiliary company for two years, performing with the ensemble at Carnegie Hall in 1941. Young Betty Bloomer thrived in the cosmopolitan atmosphere of New York and she thought seriously of relocating there permanently. Close family ties, however, began to influence her calculations. Her father had died in 1934 and her mother, now remarried, missed her daughter's company. After a series of long family discussions Betty decided to return to Grand Rapids in the late summer of 1941. She taught dance to a school age troupe and took a position as an assistant fashion coordinator at Herpolsheimer's, a locally prominent department store.

In 1942 Betty Bloomer married Bill Warren, a long-time acquaintance whom she had known since primary school. The couple moved often during the early years of their marriage as Bill Warren changed jobs often in the sales and marketing field. This semi-nomadic lifestyle seemed to suit Bill well enough, but Betty soon found it quite difficult. She returned to Grand Rapids and went back to work at Herpolsheimer's, this time as head fashion coordinator. The distance between the marriage partners, both literal and figurative, strained their union to the breaking point. The couple agreed to divorce and they parted on amicable terms in May of 1947.[11]

In the early spring of 1947 Peggy Neuman, an old friend, approached Betty on behalf of Jerry Ford, a young lawyer whose name she had heard, but who she did not know personally. Betty found out that this young attorney had been a college football star, and later a coach at Yale University. She also found that he had served with distinction as a Naval Officer in the Pacific Theater of Operations during World War II. Betty, however, remained largely unimpressed. She had little free time and her job demanded constant attention. She also frowned upon dating until the courts finalized her divorce decree. Finally, Betty had been married for five years and did not intend to plunge back into the matrimonial state too quickly. Initially she resisted Jerry Ford's amorous advances.

---

[11] Ibid.

Jerry Ford was nothing, however, if not persistent. He found Betty's wit, vivacity, and zest for life appealing and he continued to press his charm offensive, finally convincing Betty to meet him for a drink after work. The couple developed a mutual attraction but the relationship proceeded at a deliberate pace. Ford explained in his memoir that he and Betty were each too busy in their respective careers to devote a substantial amount of time to their budding romance. They dated only once or twice weekly, but they found that their attraction kept growing. Over the Christmas holidays in 1947 Ford journeyed to Sun Valley, Idaho for a ski vacation, while Betty stayed behind in Grand Rapids.[12] During this time apart Ford realized that he missed Betty terribly and his regard and feeling grew. He proposed marriage in February of 1948 and Betty accepted.

Ford informed Betty that their wedding would have to wait until the autumn, telling her, cryptically, that he "… had to do something first."[13] He had to defeat Bartel Jonkman in the Republican Congressional primary which he duly accomplished on September 14, 1948. Gerald and Betty Ford married on October 15, 1948 during the middle of the first Ford general election campaign. The couple spent their wedding night in a Detroit hotel, attended the University of Michigan-Northwestern football game the next afternoon and then promptly drove across the state to the town of Owosso to campaign with Republican Presidential candidate Thomas Dewey, the governor of New York.[14] Such was the new Mrs. Ford's introduction to life as a political spouse.

Betty Ford readily took to the role of a congressional wife of her era. She spent much of her free time involved in volunteer work with the Congressional Wives Club and the National Federation of Republican Women. She also entertained visiting dignitaries from Michigan and provided tours of the capitol building for visiting Michigan students and private citizens.[15] The Fords established a family during the congressional years, as well. The union produced four children: Michael Gerald Ford, born on March 14, 1950, followed by John Gardner Ford, (commonly known as "Jack") born on March 16, 1952, Steven Megis Ford, born on May 19, 1956, and Susan Elizabeth Ford, born on July 6, 1957. The Ford household rounded out when they hired Clara Powell to assist in general housekeeping in 1949. She worked for the

---

[12] Cannon, *Time And Chance*, P.48.
[13] Gerald R. Ford Timeline & Betty Ford Biographical Documents, found at GRFPL, Vertical File.
[14] Cannon, *Time And Chance*, p. 55-56.
[15] Ibid.

Fords and became an extended family member for the next quarter-century.[16] Following the marriage and electoral victory in 1948 the Congressman-elect and Mrs. Ford contemplated their changing fortune. They knew they would soon be moving to Washington D.C. and actually visited the district in late November, looking at rental properties. They signed a lease for a small apartment on Q Street, on the northwest side of the city. They formally moved to Washington over the New Year's holiday in 1949.

Gerald Ford found himself the very picture of obscurity as he prepared for his first congressional term. He was fond of telling the story of his near ejection from the House Office Building by the Capitol police the day he and his administrative aide, John Milanowski, arrived to clean and paint his congressional office.[17] Ford and Milanowski eventually convinced the Security Officers of their identities and credentials and went about their custodial duties without further interruption.[18] Ford also made a number of inquiries and found that he would serve on the House Public Works Committee. He took no joy in his assignment to this generally unimportant committee, although his committee membership earned him a guided tour of the White House from President Harry Truman, himself. Ford impressed many, as he had from boyhood, with his earnest manner and general decency, which, of course, masked a deceptive ambition. Ford studied his new job and the institution intently and tried to learn everything he could about the Congress. U.S. Representative Gerald R. Ford, Jr. fell back on his old football roots and devised a game plan that he stuck with for the entirety of his Congressional years. He executed the game plan by working diligently hard to advance Republican initiatives and to advance his own fortunes in the process.

During his first term Ford made the acquaintance of two ambitious fellow members who would each play fateful roles on the national stage. John F. Kennedy, the Massachusetts Democrat, worked in an office suite directly across the corridor from Ford in the House Office Building. The men got to know each other well and they walked together to the House Chambers every day. Their acquaintance gradually warmed to genuine friendship. Ford claimed later that he had no inkling of Kennedy's now documented ill health. He also recalled that he and his House colleagues had suspicions of their fellow

---

[16] Ford, *A Time To Heal*, p.68.
[17] Brinkley, *Gerald Ford*, p. 14. Also see Cannon, *Time And Chance*, p. 54.
[18] Brinkley, *Gerald R. Ford*, p. 15.

members relentless womanizing, but Ford decided, "... That was none of my business."[19]

Ford also met Richard Nixon, the up-and-coming California Republican, who made it a point of introducing himself immediately after Ford had taken his oath of office. The two men found that they had much in common. They were the same age; they were attorneys and ex-Naval officers, and former college football players. Despite great personality differences Ford and Nixon became instant friends, and remained close for the rest of their lives. They became political allies, as well, with Ford's center-right philosophy meshing well with Nixon's own generally centrist thinking, although neither man had yet carefully refined a political ideology. Together they helped to organize the "Chowder And Marching Club" an informal social society of young Republican members of the U.S. House of Representatives.

During Ford's first term he remembered one exceptionally noteworthy event. This concerned his friend Dick Nixon and his dogged investigation of former State Department official Alger Hiss, amid allegations of treason, before the House Committee on Un-American Activities.[20] Ford noted later, without commenting on the particulars of the case, that he admired his friend Nixon's ability to work his way through thousands of pages of materials and to focus his attention on the matter at hand.[21] Ford stated that this illustrated the importance of preparation, thoroughness, and plain hard work in pursuit of political goals. This Nixonian example dovetailed perfectly with Ford's own family credo concerning hard and tireless work.

In the autumn of 1950 Ford received a career boost when he secured appointment to the powerful House Appropriations Committee. U.S. Representative Albert Engel, a committee member, left Congress in order to run for the governorship of Michigan, thus leaving a Republican vacancy on the committee. In addition to residing in the same electorally important state, Ford shared Engel's general philosophy of government. The ranking Republican on the committee, John Taber of New York, tapped Ford for the

---

[19] Ibid.

[20] For the Alger Hiss case see Allen Weinstein, *Perjury: The Hiss-Chambers Case* (New York: Random House 1978, 1987). Also See, Allen Weinstein, *The Haunted Wood* (New York: Random House, 1999) and Herbert Romerstein and Eric Breindel, *The Venona Secrets: Exposing Soviet Espionage and America's Traitors* (Washington D. C. Regnery Publishing, 2000).

[21] Brinkley, *Gerald R. Ford*, p.18. Also see Cannon, *Time And Chance*, p. 55.

open seat. Ford began to develop his reputation as a fiscal conservative who scrutinized the expenditure of each dollar carefully from this point forward.[22]

Gaining a seat on the powerful Appropriations Committee proved that Ford had won the respect of his peers in Congress. While few observers saw him as a rising GOP star, most conceded that Gerald Ford had a bright political future. His straightforward nature, his hardworking habits, and understated yet, real ambition would carry him far. The Appropriations Committee seat also provided Ford with a prize bauble for his 1950 re-election campaign. His victory was a near certainty in a heavily Republican district like Western Michigan and landing the highly coveted seat on the Appropriations Committee clinched the deal. In November, Congressman Ford won re-election in the 5th Michigan Congressional District, taking over 66% of the vote. It was the first of Ford's twelve successful re-election campaigns and Congressman Ford never garnered less than 60% of the total vote.

During the 1950s Congressman Ford built his political base and his reputation. Ford's earnest nature, his genuine nice-guy persona, and his indefatigable work habits earned him credit among his colleagues. He carefully concealed a competitive nature and a keen ambition, made many friends, and surprisingly few enemies along the way. The Democrats controlled Congress for all but one of Ford's terms, so his ability to initiate and advance legislation remained limited. He did, however, exercise growing influence on the Appropriations Committee, where he briefly (1953-54) chaired the Defense Appropriations Subcommittee and the Army Panel. In 1957-58 Ford served on the "Select Committee on Astronautics and Space Exploration," chaired by Lyndon Johnson, the Democratic Senator from Texas. This committee, formed in response to the Soviet Union's launch of a space satellite on October 4, 1957, recommended the creation of the National Aeronautics and Space Administration.

Where did Gerald Ford stand on the great issues of his age? Ford had established his center-right proclivities early in his congressional career, but a closer examination of the record during the 1950s indicates that Congressman Gerald Ford hewed much closer to the center than to the right. Ford, true to his internationalist declarations, supported the Marshall Plan and President Truman's Point Four program providing financial assistance to underdeveloped countries, increases in the U.S. defense budget, and general support for foreign aid. He opposed the repeal of the Taft-Hartley Act, and voted against an increase in the minimum wage. He also voted to override

---

[22] Ford, A Time To Heal, p. 70.

President Truman's veto of the McCarran Internal Security Act of 1951. Ford preferred, though, to avoid taking an active role in many of the contentious issues of the time.

In his autobiography Ford claimed that the greatest regret of his early congressional years was his failure to speak out against the excesses of Senator Joseph McCarthy, the crusading anti-communist Republican from Wisconsin.[23] Ford said that he disliked McCarthy personally and should have spoken out in opposition to the Senator and his supposedly reckless accusations, but chose to remain silent. He did not elaborate on this theme in his memoir or any later writings and a one-sentence condemnation of a singularly unpopular politician twenty years after his death might well be dismissed as self-serving and sanctimonious. Ford stayed out of the fray on the domestic communist issue and, like many moderate politicians of the age, he hoped that the controversy would fade away over time.

Another example of Congressman Ford's centrist bent is the fact that he joined with nineteen other young Republican legislators in sending a formal letter to General Dwight D. Eisenhower in February of 1952, urging him to pursue the Republican nomination for the Presidency of the United States.[24] Ford insisted that he preferred Eisenhower over Senator Robert Taft of Ohio, the early frontrunner, because of Eisenhower's internationalist foreign policy agenda. Senator Taft generally exemplified the classic Midwestern non-interventionist foreign policy that motivated Ford to challenge the isolationist congressional incumbent Bartel Jonkman in 1948, but Eisenhower's own foreign policy views remained largely unknown in early 1952. Gerald Ford, and the other signers of the letter very likely saw the erstwhile war hero as a sure winner and, like professional politicians, they saw victory as the highest good. Ford, tending toward moderation rather than conservatism, required no convincing on this score. He supported a center-right dream candidate rather than a dyed-in-the-wool conservative who might conceivably have lost in a general election.

Ford, himself, made a number of momentous decisions during the "Fabulous Fifties." Shortly after arriving in Congress, Ford decided that his ultimate goal was to win the House Speakership, and he set about researching a way to achieve this goal. Ford studied the careers of legendary figures like James K. Polk, Thomas B. Reed and Joe Cannon, as well as House leaders closer to his own era. He made overtures to each Party faction, moved

---

[23] Ibid.
[24] Gerald Ford Timeline, found at GRFPL, Vertical File.

cautiously, and tried to avoid creating enemies. Meanwhile, as Ford built his reputation, his friends in the Michigan Republican Party, pleased with his service, sought him out and urged him to seek higher office.[25] He declined to run for the U.S. Senate in 1954 and refused his associates again over a possible gubernatorial run in 1956.[26] In fact, Ford ran for higher office only in 1976, when seeking to hold the Presidency of the United States.

Why did this popular and promising legislator eschew a run for higher office? In his writings Ford declared that he wanted no position other than the House Speakership. On the surface this may have been true, although Ford accepted the Vice-Presidency when the Party needed him in 1973. His reluctance to seek higher office probably stemmed from a number of motives, some political and some personal. Gerald Ford enjoyed his time in the House of Representatives.[27] The sense of collegial masculinity marking Congress in those years took Ford back to his roots as a coach, a college football star, and a Big-Man-On-Campus in college. He reveled in this environment and impressed everyone with his winning personality. Secondly, Ford knew that he represented a safely Republican congressional seat. He served his district and his constituents well and knew that he would win re-election easily, barring a political earthquake. Here his innate cautiousness came into play. Ford realized that he could not coast to victory in a statewide political race. He realized that he might, in fact, lose a contest for the U.S. Senate or the Michigan governorship. Ford's appeal in the small cities and rural areas of Western Michigan might have translated poorly in Detroit and the eastern half of the state. Could Gerald Ford's moderate conservatism have attracted African-American voters in Detroit? Ford's tacit support for the Taft-Hartley Act would have proven a tough sell to the large blue-collar labor vote in Eastern Michigan, although many ethnic Democrats would have looked favorably upon his anti-Soviet stance. It is entirely possible that Ford declined to seek higher elective office because he suspected he would lose a statewide race. He chose to remain in the House of Representatives, where his reputation served him well, his hard work earned him credit, and his lack of charisma hurt very little.

In early 1959 Ford joined with a group of fellow Republicans in a move to oust the Party's House leader, Massachusetts Congressman Joe Martin, and to

---

[25] Ibid.
[26] Author interviews with Lee Edwards, November 19, 2009 and Steven Hayward, November 20, 2009.
[27] Brinkley, *Gerald R. Ford*, pp. 20-23.

replace him with Charles Halleck of Indiana. Ford certainly stepped out of character in this instance, as he dropped his nice-guy, Party loyalist demeanor and conspired with an insurgent group to depose Joe Martin. Ford and his co-conspirators believed that Martin and the GOP House leadership had grown complacent and stale and they further thought that the full Party needed fresh and decisive leadership. At the close of 1958, following a serious Republican defeat in the mid-term elections of the previous November, the cabal began secretly plotting to oust Martin, a genial ex-newspaper publisher, who had directed the GOP in the House of Representatives for twenty years.

In Ford's own words the Republican Party absorbed a "terrible beating" in the 1958 midterm elections.[28] The economy took a nosedive during the fourth quarter of 1957 and the New Year, 1958, opened with the country undergoing a serious recession. The public vented frustration at the ballot box in November and the Democrats enlarged their already substantial majorities in both chambers of the national legislature. Ford conceded that the troubled economy had sunk the Party at the polls, but he also believed that the entire GOP organization projected an aged and tired image. Ford and a number of his House colleagues spoke frankly to Joe Martin and told him that he needed to step aside for the good of the Party. They explained to Martin that he should leave his position and assume an unofficial role as an elder statesman. Martin refused to allow himself to be kicked upstairs and decided to fight. He knew that the plain speaking Indiana Representative Charles Halleck led the insurgent group and he appealed to Gerald Ford for support, noting Ford's reputation as a loyal Party man. Despite Martin's personal appeal, Ford cast his lot with Halleck and the insurgent faction, and they voted Martin out on January 6, 1959. Charles Halleck served as the Republican leader in the house for the next six years; he was forced out on January 4, 1965 by his one-time ally, Congressman Gerald R. Ford.

In these instances Ford displayed a Machiavellian streak that he usually concealed behind his genial, nice-guy image. Ford had developed his reputation as the consummate Party man by accepting the direction of Party leaders and generally adhering to the standard line. He showed, in 1958, however, that he was now a power in the national GOP and his actions in helping to oust Charles Halleck after another GOP electoral debacle in 1964 showed that he could willingly engage in old fashioned political infighting, double dealing, and dirty tricks if he considered them appropriate to a given political situation.

---

[28] Ford, *A Time to Heal*, p. 72.

During the 50s Ford's friendship with Richard Nixon continued and deepened, although their friendship more often resembled a political alliance than a traditional male fellowship and camaraderie. Ford invited Nixon to Grand Rapids to give the keynote speech at the Lincoln Day Dinner in 1951.[29] Nixon spent the night at the Ford family home. Five years later Ford defended Nixon when certain disgruntled Republicans weighed the possibility of dumping him off of the national ticket prior to the 1956 elections. Finally, in 1960 Ford publicly committed his early support to Nixon for the Republican presidential nomination. Ford and his center-rightist Republican friends wanted a candidate who could win the upcoming election and keep the White House in GOP hands and they supported Nixon on that basis. Ford could have happily backed New York Governor Nelson Rockefeller, but a shrewd political calculation showed that Rockefeller did not match up well with the prospective Democratic nominees. Also, by 1960 the GOP felt the first tremors of a tectonic shift in party make-up and positioning, as the Party's conservative wing grew restless and demanding. Nelson Rockefeller was simply unacceptable to the Republican right wing and Ford, always sensitive to potential career damaging controversy, steered clear of the Rockefeller camp by endorsing his old friend Dick Nixon, even though President Eisenhower seemed somewhat cool in support of his Vice-President for the top job.[30]

Rockefeller provided the only real challenge to Nixon in the 1960 primary season. The two men shared a mutual disdain with Nixon particularly resenting Rockefeller because of his inherited wealth, pedigree and social status. The antipathy between the two men was so strong that it threatened Party unity in the upcoming general election. During the Republican convention Nixon aides hastily arranged a meeting with Rockefeller at the governor's New York City penthouse. Rockefeller agreed to support Nixon's nomination and to campaign for the GOP ticket in the fall. In exchange, Nixon and his team agreed to allow Rockefeller a significant role in writing the Party's 1960 platform.[31] This agreement smoothed troubled Party waters, but infuriated Republican conservatives and their champion, Arizona Senator Barry Goldwater, who had long suspected Nixon and his deceitful ways.

---

[29] Gerald Ford Timeline, found at GRFPL, Vertical File.
[30] Brinkley, *Gerald R. Ford*, pp. 22.
[31] Lee Edwards, *The Conservative Revolution: The Movement that Remade America*, (New York: Simon & Schuster, 1999) pp. 91-92. Also see, James T. Patterson, *Grand Expectations: The United States, 1945-1974*, (New York: Oxford University Press, 1996) pp. 435-438.

During the run-up to the GOP convention influential Michigan Republicans began circulating Gerald Ford's name as a possible Nixon running mate. The presumptive Presidential nominee encouraged this speculation, since Ford enjoyed nearly universal respect in Party circles. Ford appealed to most of the Party subgroups, having fashioned a conservative voting record on most fiscal issues, and a dependable Party-line stand on world affairs. Ford's moderate stance on civil rights and labor relations, combined with his roots in electorally important Michigan served to enhance his status as a potential Vice-Presidential candidate.[32]

The historical record concerning the Ford for Vice-President boomlet in 1960 is unclear. When Congressman and Mrs. Gerald R. Ford arrived at Chicago's Midway Airport prior to the Party's July convention they met dozens of cheering supporters waving "Ford for Vice-President" signs. Ford said little about this in his generally uninformative autobiography, except to acknowledge the fact that his name was mentioned and that he would have been receptive to Party overtures. In any event, the GOP strategists concluded that Ford would best serve the Party by remaining in Congress and declined to push his Vice-Presidential nomination. The reasoning behind this decision started with the proposition that Ford brought little to the ticket. His center-right views appealed to likely Republican voters, but would have brought few independents into the Nixon fold. As Douglas Brinkley put it, "... So Nixon passed over his friend Jerry Ford, instead asking him to make the seconding speech for the Vice-Presidential nomination of Boston Brahmin Henry Cabot Lodge, who brought diplomatic experience and Cold War credentials to the ticket."[33] Ford, ever the loyal Republican soldier, swallowed any disappointment he may have experienced and gave the speech for Henry Cabot Lodge, just as requested.

Ford nevertheless played an active role in the 1960 campaign. His re-election was a virtual certainty, as he had represented his district for twelve years and had never faced a serious challenge. Ford's own employment future secure, he could take an active role campaigning around the country for GOP candidates and issues. The Nixon team decided that Ford could help the cause by joining two fellow Republican congressional members and follow Democratic nominee John F. Kennedy on the campaign trail answering the Massachusetts Senator's claims and assertions.[34] The Republican "Truth

---

[32] Brinkley, *Gerald R. Ford*, pp. 21-22. Also see, Cannon, *Time And Chance*, p. 68.
[33] Brinkley, *Gerald R. Ford*, p. 22.
[34] Ibid. p. 23

Squad" failed to play a major role in the 1960 election, although Ford found that he enjoyed the experience immensely. Ford believed that his close friend Nixon would defeat his old friend and fellow Congressman Kennedy in the election. The agonizingly close popular vote and the controversial nature of the tallies in Illinois, Texas, and Alabama breaking in favor of Kennedy served to dishearten Ford and his fellow Republicans. Of course, Ford and his colleagues consoled themselves with the knowledge that Kennedy's Democratic victory was largely personal in nature. The Republicans gained twenty seats in the House and two Senate seats in the electoral tilt. Ford and his GOP mates settled in, prepared for the Kennedy Administration, and like good politicians, began looking forward to the next election.

Chapter 5

MOVING ON UP: 1961-1972

As Gerald Ford, his fellow politicians, and the American people passed the final weeks of 1960 and the interregnum, awaiting the inauguration of President-Elect John F. Kennedy a student of history wonders if the public understood the momentous nature of the changes then afoot in America, and the world. Did people realize that they were witnessing the end of a social, cultural, and political era? In the realm of American politics there is no doubt that petty partisan bickering marked the Eisenhower years, as partisan wrangling marks every era, but, this tiresome constant masked a general consensus and a unity of purpose seldom seen in American politics, before or since. The Eisenhower Age could rightly be referred to as a twentieth century "Era of Good Feelings" harkening back to the original 1817-1825 period when the nation tried to overlook brewing trouble and, instead, concentrated on accentuating the positives in American life. Eisenhower, himself, had offered a stabilizing compass point for the country, and most of the people saw a bright future ahead.[1]

The Eisenhower Age seemed placid and tranquil and, while Ike offered little in the way of charismatic leadership, he presented a seemingly steady hand on the helm of state. In truth, though, the nation was changing at a breakneck pace and the slight rumble of growing unrest (already evident in problematic racial difficulties) would explode into drastic, often violent upheaval in the 1960s. Modern historians part company when discussing and trying to explain this phenomenon. There is no consensus on when and how this began and historians differ on the ultimate significance of these changes.

---

[1] For a generally favorable view of the 1950s see Jeffrey Hart, *When The Going Was Good: American Life in the Fifties,* (New York: Crown Press, 1982).

Some commentators see these changes as largely beneficial, while others condemn the 1960s and the so-called "New Left" as having had a bad, even disastrous effect on American society.[2] In fact, while it is historically inaccurate to describe the 1950s as universally tranquil, placid, and "conservative" it would be equally inaccurate to describe the 1960s as entirely radical, rebellious, and nihilistic. Radicalism did rear its head, particularly in the supposed "youth rebellion" later in the decade, but many Americans continued to live life as they had before, and the sensible center held, in most respects. Still, few Americans would deny that the country changed dramatically between 1961-1972.

Where was Gerald R. Ford on the eve of these historic changes? Ford, having steadily moved upward in his Republican Party, now settled in as the ranking minority member on the House Defense Appropriations Subcommittee. Gerald Ford was no visionary, and he probably remained unaware of the winds of change that were beginning to buffet American society. During the 1960s and early 1970s Ford applied himself to his responsibilities with the diligence that had become his trademark. He usually remained a steadfast Party man, although he supported some of President Kennedy's initiatives on foreign aid and the space race.[3] The American Political Science Association recognized Ford's growing stature when they named him as the winner of their Congressional Distinguished Service Award, in 1961. The awards committee called Ford "A Congressman's Congressman," and lauded him for his indefatigable work habits and his mastery of the complexities of the legislative process.

Calendar year 1962 proved a significant annum for Gerald Ford. On January 26th his stepfather, Gerald R. Ford, Sr. died in Grand Rapids at the age of 72. Dorothy Gardner Ford, the congressman's mother, continued to live in the family home, while drawing financial assistance from her four sons until her death at the age of 75 on September 17, 1967.[4] Politically speaking, calendar year 1962 turned out somewhat disappointingly for Ford and his Republican colleagues. The GOP leaders fully expected to gain seats in both Houses of Congress in the midterm elections in November. Their optimism

---

[2] See Maurice Isserman & Michael Kazin, *America Divided: The Civil War of the 1960s* (New York: Oxford University Press, 2004) for a generally favorable treatment of the New Left. For a more critical view of the New Left, see Roger Kimball, *The Long March: How The Cultural Revolution of the 1960s Changed America*, (San Francisco: Encounter Books, 2000).

[3] Ford Timeline Documents, found at GRFPL, Vertical File.

[4] Ibid.

sprang from the fact that President Kennedy's 1960 victory was largely personal in nature. JFK brought no Democratic wave into Congress with him. He essentially provided no "coattail effect" as the Republicans actually increased their numbers in Congress in the 1960 general election. Also, the Republican leadership grasped the historical tradition that the Party holding the Presidency usually loses legislative seats during the midterm elections. Thus the Grand Old Party optimistically approached the 1962 campaign, expecting good tidings.

Unfortunately, for the Republicans, the expected gains failed to materialize. President Kennedy, showing resolve and diplomatic shrewdness, successfully defused the Cuban missile confrontation with the Soviet Union, in October. He brought credit to himself and his somewhat untested Administration and, this success, combined with the American tradition of rallying around the President in times of national emergency helped the Democrats to gain two seats in the Senate. The Republicans consoled themselves with the knowledge that they did pick up one seat in the House but given the Republican pre-election enthusiasm they did rather poorly. Ford easily won his seventh re-election campaign, but he admitted in his memoirs that he took the national election results particularly hard.

In January of 1963 a faction of younger Republican Congressmen led by Charles Goodell of New York, Robert Griffin of Michigan, Melvin Laird of Wisconsin, and Donald Rumsfeld of Illinois, urged Ford to challenge Charles Hoeven of Iowa for House Republican Conference Chairman.[5] Ford agreed that the Party required fresher and more assertive leadership, so he agreed to challenge Hoeven and duly defeated him in a GOP caucus vote.[6] Hoeven did not accept his defeat graciously and warned House Republican leader Charles Halleck to watch his back, informing him that Ford would ultimately attempt to "steal" the Minority Leader position.[7]

Ford and his colleagues resumed their labors in 1963, unaware that the calendar cycle would go into the books as one of the most tragic years in all of American history. On November 22, 1963 President John F. Kennedy was assassinated during a pre-Thanksgiving political trip to Dallas, Texas. Ford recalled in his memoirs that he heard the dreadful news on his car radio in the early afternoon. Exactly one week later, on November 29th the newly sworn-in President Lyndon B. Johnson appointed Ford to a seven-man committee to

---

[5] Brinkley, *Gerald R. Ford*, p. 23. Also see, Cannon, *Time And Chance*, pp. 73-75.
[6] Ford Timeline Documents, found at GRFPL, Vertical File.
[7] Ibid.

investigate the Kennedy assassination. The commission, headed by Supreme Court Chief Justice Earl Warren, and known informally as the "Warren Commission" was comprised of three Democrats, three Republicans, and the supposedly non-partisan chief jurist. Ford considered the appointment an honor, but in reality he worried that it would place demands on his already limited time. In addition to his new duties chairing the House Republican Caucus, Ford held the ranking minority seat on the House Appropriations Committee, and held responsibilities on other committees, as well. He solved his time problem by assigning a considerable amount of preparatory work to his staff aides Jack Stiles and Bob Hartman. They reviewed much of the primary material and summarized various intricacies so that Ford could tackle these issues during meetings.[8]

Ford claimed in his autobiography that he butted heads with Chief Justice Warren over the direction of the investigation, but that they settled most of their differences amicably.[9] In point of fact, Ford accompanied Warren to Dallas on an investigative trip in which they re-created the actual assassination. On September 27, 1964 the Commission published their findings, reporting that they found no evidence to suggest that a conspiracy existed to murder President Kennedy. Ford and his investigative assistant Jack Stiles later published their own book *Portrait of an Assassin*, as a way of underscoring and reinforcing the commission report.

As Johnson took the helm in 1963 the Republicans were forced to adjust to a new President whose demeanor, style, and operational manner differed markedly from his immediate predecessor. President Johnson pushed an ambitious legislative agenda and kept his GOP opponents off balance for the remainder of his inherited term. Johnson's disdain for his political rivals was already an established fact by the time he became President and he mocked Jerry Ford scornfully, reportedly stating "Jerry Ford is so dumb he can't fart and chew gum at the same time"[10] and adding, "Jerry Ford is a nice fellow but he spent too much time playing football without a helmet."[11] Ford publicly ignored such barbs, but he privately returned Johnson's antipathy and disliked the President, although he kept negative judgments to himself. Ford realized, sensibly, that contemptuous remarks about the President would poison the atmosphere and turn ordinary politics into blood sport, helping no one. Ford, a

---

[8] Cannon, *Time And Chance*, pp. 75-78.
[9] Ford, *A Time To Heal*, pp. 74-75.
[10] Cannon, *Time And Chance*, pp. 93-94.
[11] Ibid.

master practitioner of consensus politics, insisted on keeping himself and his Party faction above the sordid business of character assassination.

The nation faced a general election in 1964 and the Democrats sensed victory in the air. They planned, naturally, to ride the wave of national sympathy following Kennedy's meaningless assassination back into the White House for four more years, and they hoped to broaden their Congressional majorities, as well. President Johnson, the certain Democratic nominee, proved to be a tough and shrewd candidate, even though his limitations as the national leader became more apparent. The Republican Party, on the other hand, waged a bitter internecine battle between rival factions. The Party and its moderate Eastern establishment lined up behind New York Governor Nelson Rockefeller, while the conservative wing, made up mostly of Westerners and the few Southerners who publicly supported the Republican Party promoted Arizona Senator Barry Goldwater, as their somewhat reluctant champion. In his memoir Ford lamented the fact that, "Since 1960, the Party had swung to the right. Zealots had taken over key positions and they seemed to believe that it was more important to nominate a candidate who was ideologically pure than to find someone who could win an election."[12] Ford clearly blamed the purportedly reckless conservatives for tearing the GOP apart and leading the Party to a Waterloo-like defeat in November of 1964. Many modern political historians echo Ford's judgment, but it would be a mistake to oversimplify this turn of events. The Republican Party experienced the first tremors of a tectonic shift in the American political paradigm in 1964. As the political journalist William Rusher said, "… it is clear, in retrospect, that Ford simply had no comprehension of the seismic forces at work in American politics."[13] As the political scientist Kevin Phillips would note in his 1968 volume, *The Emerging Republican Majority*, the entire structure of the American political and electoral coalition was now in flux and many traditional Democratic constituencies were now leaning in a Republican direction. Gerald R. Ford, a practical politician of considerable repute and skill, proved once again to be no visionary and did not grasp the nature or the import of these paradigm shifts.

The Goldwater-Rockefeller face-off forced nearly every prominent Republican to take a stand and left few able to straddle the fence. In choosing sides many Republican politicians irrevocably committed their loyalty to a Party faction, thereby alienating the other bloc in the process. The

---

[12] Ford, *A Time to Heal*, p. 77; Cannon, *Time And Chance*, pp. 93-94.

[13] William Rusher, *The Rise of the Right*, (New York: William Morrow & Company, 1984) p. 264.

Goldwaterites immediately earned the enmity of the GOP moderate-liberal coalition and later found themselves blamed for the 1964 electoral thrashing. The Rockefeller supporters sensed, correctly, that the conservatives were testing their dominance of the Party and they resisted this challenge for many reasons, primarily fearing that the conservatives would drown the GOP in a general election tidal wave. The 1964 election results seemed to confirm these fears.

Where did U.S. Representative Gerald R. Ford stand in this potentially career damaging battle? Ford showed remarkable foresight and no small amount of dexterity in successfully negotiating this minefield. He finessed, although some would say he "ducked," the entire issue by publicly supporting his fellow Michigander, Governor George Romney, as a favorite-son candidate.[14] Ford knew that Romney could not win the nomination, but in supporting the Romney candidacy Ford nimbly dodged the moderate-conservative brushfire, thereby immunizing himself against future recriminations. In 1964 Ford showed a healthy level of political self-calculation, one that he rarely demonstrated, as political escape artistry was not his stock-in-trade. He did, however, manage to steer clear of the dangerous shoals of lining up with the "wrong" faction, and he came through the 1964 crucible handsomely.

Unfortunately, the same could not be said of Ford's beloved Republican Party. While Ford easily won re-election to his ninth congressional term, the Democrats handed the Republicans a brutal shellacking across the country on Election Day. The Democrats captured the Presidency, with Johnson taking 61% of the popular vote and 44 states.[15] The senior Party also increased their majorities in both chambers of Congress, and retained their hold on most state governorships and legislative houses. Republican strategists could find few bright spots amidst the wreckage, except to note that the Deep South, the most solidly Democratic region of the country, broke decisively for Goldwater and the Republicans this time around.[16]

The GOP congressional delegation, convinced that they needed more vigorous leadership, began considering a change at the top of the Party. Jerry Ford leaned in this direction and, after tactical meetings with a number of colleagues namely Robert Griffin of Michigan, Charles Goodell of New York, and Donald Rumsfeld of Illinois, he announced that he would challenge

---

[14] Cannon, *Time And Chance*, p. 78. Also see, Ford, *A Time To Heal*, p. 77.
[15] Patterson, *Grand Expectations*, p. 561.
[16] Ibid.

Charles Halleck for the position of House Minority (Republican) Leader. Ford duly won the position in a surprisingly close 73-67 caucus vote on January 4, 1965.[17] Ford credited Kansas Congressman Bob Dole for his victory, noting that Dole had offered his support and brought in all five of the Kansas Republicans with him. Jerry Ford and Bob Dole became good friends from this moment forward and in the coming years their political futures would certainly intertwine, as well.

The Democrats resounding victory in 1964 resulted in more than simple numerical difficulties for the outmanned GOP. Ford related his forebodings in his memoirs saying that President Johnson found the victory personally exhilarating and saw it as a mandate for an ambitious legislative agenda. Johnson, somewhat personally insecure, hoped to prove his liberal bonafides by pursuing an avowed progressive agenda, and hoped to illustrate his mastery of the legislative process by shepherding a liberal program through Congress, something that John F. Kennedy had found impossible.[18] Minority Leader Ford could only count 140 Party members and realized that the heavy Democratic majorities working at Johnson's behest meant tough sledding for the Republican Party in the next four years.

Gradually, the GOP leadership devised a strategy to offer alternatives to Johnson's Democrats and what they referred to as the "Great Society." Ford, the non-ideologue, did express his fears at this time that the federal government was growing too large, too complex, too intrusive and above all, too expensive. In these criticisms Ford certainly lined up with traditional Republican themes and ideas. He understood, though, that political realities required the GOP to offer real alternatives. The Republicans could criticize, delay, and hold but needed, at some point, to offer a positive vision for the country. During 1965–66 Ford offered Republican counterproposals to the Great Society legislation. He also began to appear with Senate Minority Leader Everett Dirksen of Illinois in weekly press conferences critiquing the Johnson Administration. These televised appearances became known colloquially as "The Ev and Jerry Show" and served a useful purpose in spreading the Republican message in a mass media age. President Johnson, an intensely proud man who took criticism personally, resented these attacks and petulantly answered the GOP jabs with zingers of his own.

Lyndon Johnson and the Democrats made good on many of their campaign promises in the 1965-66 Congressional session. President Johnson's

---

[17] Ford Timeline Documents, found at GRFPL, Vertical File
[18] Ford, *A Time to Heal*, p. 77.

Party passed a comprehensive civil rights bill and established the groundwork for the Great Society, broadening federal responsibility in many theretofore untouched areas. Though the Democrats legislative victories were impressive, no one could question the rising level of tension in America at the same time. The Great Society programs proved as costly as Ford and his Republican allies had predicted and government spending increased markedly. Despite passage of the civil rights bill simmering racial unrest boiled over into bitter race riots in Los Angeles, Detroit, and Newark in 1965. Many Americans also began to express misgivings over a complex and largely misunderstood conflict in Southeast Asia, which by 1966 had begun to soak up a significant portion of government resources and resulted in ever-increasing casualty lists.

Jerry Ford vigorously stumped the country on behalf of Republican candidates during the midterm election campaign in the autumn of 1966. The Republicans sensed political opportunity and intended to capitalize, if possible. While the GOP rode a wave of voter dissatisfaction to political benefit, shrewder observers sensed that the storm gathering in the country involved more than ordinary politics. It involved a full conflict of socio-cultural visions and represented the first skirmish in what would become a complete ideological tumult. In any event, the Republicans won a startlingly strong electoral victory in the November 8, 1966 elections.[19] They gained 12 seats in the Senate and a full 47 in the House of Representatives. Gerald R. Ford won his tenth election with 68% of the vote, the largest re-election margin of his long career.

In his second term as House Minority Leader, Ford led his GOP troops in continued delaying actions against Democratic attempts to expand the Great Society. Ford demonstrated his pragmatic-centrist bent in these matters by insisting that his Party had to offer alternatives to the Democratic proposals.[20] He believed that simple negativity would ultimately prove destructive to the Republicans and that they needed to be a Party of ideas, even if he himself, was not an "idea man." In practice, many Republican alternatives proved to be watered down versions of the Democratic proposals and critics began to refer to this as "Me Too-Republicanism", meaning that the GOP accepted the general Democratic premise on a certain issue, but that they promised to keep tighter reins on the purse strings than the rival Party. Ford, understanding this criticism, pushed for alternative proposals regardless of their ideological origins, supporting the positions of certain liberals in the Party, like Charles

---

[19] Ford Timeline Documents, found at GRFPL, Vertical file.
[20] Ford, *A Time To Heal*, p. 80.

Goodell of New York, as well as the ideas of center-rightists like Bob Dole. Ford urged the various Party factions to keep their cool and to remember that they were all playing for the same team.

Also in his second term as Minority Leader, Ford introduced an unofficial GOP policy of criticizing Johnson and the Democrats over the apparent deadlock in Vietnam. In an August 7, 1967 speech on the conflict, Ford asked the question: "Why are we pulling our best punches in Southeast Asia?"[21] While the Republicans stopped short of offering a comprehensive plan to win the war, they certainly sensed the shifting public opinion on the conflict, and sought to turn this increasing discontent to partisan advantage. Ford and his GOP allies would soon discover that political grandstanding on hot-button issues could backfire and that these tactics, effective though they might have been, would be used against them to dangerous effect in the early 70s.

On civil rights and the entire question of race in American life, Ford seemed content to follow rather than lead, generally reflecting the Republican Party and its uncertainties on the issue. Ford usually supported civil rights measures during roll call votes, although he often opposed them at the inception, usually arguing against the supposedly ruinous costs involved and working against a constantly expanding federal governmental sphere in the social realm. He drew criticism from the NAACP and the traditional civil rights establishment for his questionable commitment to their agenda, but they never worked to defeat Gerald Ford, and, more importantly, they never considered him their foe.

At length the calendar turned to 1968 and the fourth-year American general election ritual. The year 1968 promised significant change, for it was no ordinary election year. President Johnson surprised the country in late March when he announced that he would drop his re-election campaign and use the remainder of his term in office seeking to end the war in Vietnam. Johnson's decision caught most political veterans off guard, and most chalked it up to the fact that the President had survived an unexpectedly tough challenge from Minnesota Senator Eugene McCarthy in the New Hampshire Democratic primary election. While the political implications of McCarthy's challenge disconcerted the White House, Johnson's declining health also figured heavily in his decision to retire from public life.[22] The Presidential race would now be wide open and the Republicans sensed a great opportunity to win back the White House, and possibly the Congress, as well. Minority

---

[21] Ford Timeline Documents, found at GRFPL, Vertical File
[22] Patterson, *Great Expectations*, pp. 683-685.

Leader Ford sensed that 1968 was the year he would finally realize his grand political ambition, namely winning election to the Speakership of the House of Representatives.

The first important matter for the Party was deciding on a Presidential ticket for the fall campaign. The 1964 debacle loomed large in the memories of the Party veterans and they agreed that their ticket must have a realistic chance of victory. Furthermore, the politicos decided ideological purity should not detract from the ultimate goal of victory as the 1968 Presidential derby opened. Old Republican warhorse Richard Milhouse Nixon soon emerged as the clear GOP favorite. Nixon rose, Phoenix-like, from the ashes of his near Presidential miss of 1960, and his unexpected defeat in the California gubernatorial election in 1962 to lead the GOP pack, after drawing an early endorsement from Barry Goldwater in the fall of 1965. Nixon skillfully played the game, calling in favors and chits of gratitude he had built up in over twenty years of national electoral politics. He knew all of the important figures in the Party and used them to his advantage. Nixon also showed a sure grasp of the issues, a remarkably retentive memory, and an encyclopedic knowledge of foreign affairs. On the debit side, however, Nixon still harbored his well-known dislike of the media, he had made real enemies in the Democratic Party, and a sizable number of his fellow Republicans distrusted him. He also failed to generate much real enthusiasm in the country, at large, since many people tended to consider him yesterday's news.

During the Republican primary season Nixon, knowing how to work the Party machinery, jumped out to an early lead. George Romney, the governor of Michigan, ran well near the beginning, but fizzled as the campaign wore on, and Nixon padded his lead. California Governor Ronald Reagan, expressing conservative dissatisfaction with Nixon's ideological indeterminacy, committed to the race, but too late to prevent Nixon's first ballot nomination.

Gerald R. Ford presided over the 1968 Republican National Convention, held in Miami Beach. The Republicans wanted to avoid a replay of the tumultuous Democratic convention at Chicago earlier in the summer, and they succeeded, producing a model of decorum at their own gathering.[23] The Democratic Party split between their regular candidate, Vice-President Hubert Humphrey, and their rebellious southern wing led by Alabama Governor George Wallace, who deserted the Party to run on the American Independent Party ticket, gave the GOP a golden opportunity to win back the Presidency. The Party leaders debated on whom to nominate as Nixon's Vice-Presidential

---

[23] Brinkley, *Gerald R. Ford*, pp. 32-33. Also see, Cannon, *Time And Chance*, pp. 94-96.

running mate, and the presumptive Presidential nominee refused to tip his hand early. He discussed the nomination with Ford, but the House Minority Leader declared that he favored John Lindsay, the mayor of New York City, for the position.[24] In backing Lindsay for the Vice-Presidential slot, Ford played a pragmatic political game. Lindsay, a liberal Republican, in the process of wrecking the New York City municipal government, certainly shared few of Ford's center-right inclinations. Ford, however, being non-ideological in nature, wanted to win the 1968 election and hoped that Lindsay's supposed telegenic charm might add a measure of needed charisma, otherwise missing from the GOP ticket.

During meetings with Nixon and his staff, Ford personally argued on Lindsay's behalf, but the Presidential nominee surprised nearly everyone by naming the largely unknown Maryland Governor, Spiro T. Agnew, as his running mate. In his memoir, Ford admitted his shock at this development. No one could offer a logical reason for Nixon's decision. It seems likely, in historical retrospect, that Nixon wanted someone who would serve as his loyal number-two man, would hew the White House line, and would not outshine the boss.[25]

In contrast to Republican expectations, the 1968 campaign proved to be a nail biter. Many of the pre-election surveys showed the GOP ticket comfortably ahead, as the Democratic split and the supposed alienation of the youth vote worked against the senior party. The race tightened considerably in late October, as many uncommitted Democrats came home to the Party, particularly after presidential candidate Hubert Humphrey and his running mate, Maine Senator Edmund Muskie, came out in favor of immediately ending the war in Vietnam. The candidates entered the final weekend of the campaign locked in a virtual dead heat.

On Tuesday, November 4, 1968 the Nixon-Agnew ticket won a breathtakingly close general election victory. The Republican ticket took 43.4% of the popular vote to the Humphrey-Muskie ticket's 42.7%. Independent candidate George Wallace polled 13.5% of the vote, while other minor candidates split the remainder. The GOP won the Electoral College by a deceptively comfortable margin of 303-191, with 46 votes going to George Wallace, as he won the Deep South. The Republicans rejoiced in their victory, but, while they reclaimed the Presidency, the Party gained only a handful of

---

[24] Cannon, *Time And Chance*, p. 94.
[25] Edwards, *The Conservative Revolution*, pp. 61-65. Also see, Steven Hayward, *The Age of Reagan: The Fall of the Old Liberal Order: 1964-1980*, (Crown Publishing: Roseville, Ca. 2001) p. 212.

seats in the Congress.[26] Gerald Ford would remain the House Minority Leader for at least two more years. Most disturbing for GOP strategists was the stark fact that nearly 57% of the electorate had voted against the Republican ticket in the 1968 election.

Richard Nixon took the oath of office as the thirty-seventh President of the United States on January 20, 1969 alternately proud, yet strangely troubled. He reveled in his personal victory, finally winning the ultimate American political prize, a number of years after his critics had pronounced his political obituary. Still, Nixon could not forget that he was "... the first President to come into office with the opposition controlling both houses of Congress in 120 years."[27] House Minority Leader Ford consistently supported the Administration's programs and tried to help navigate the treacherous waters of congressional politics. He encouraged the Administration's "peace with honor" approach to the now thoroughly unpopular Vietnam War, and softened his Cold Warrior credentials when the Nixon State Department, confronting new domestic attitudes, pursued a conciliatory policy with the Soviet Union and China. Ford led the continued Republican effort to trim social welfare programs but, at the Administration's request, he dropped his formerly ironclad opposition to government meddling in the marketplace by accepting wage-and-price controls as part of a comprehensive anti-inflation program.[28]

Gerald Ford certainly held up his end of the bargain by supporting the Nixon program during the first term, but found that his hard work and loyalty rarely merited reciprocation from the President or his staff. In fact, Ford found the Administration puzzlingly closed, secretive, and even dismissive concerning Congressional relations. Ford maintained a cordial relationship with his old friend President Nixon, but found the boss surrounded by a coterie of staff members who expressed open contempt for the GOP Congressional leadership. John Ehrlichman, the White House Domestic Policy director, stated, "... I found Gerry Ford the type who would have made a moderately successful Grand Rapids insurance man, but he wasn't very bright."[29] The Administration made no effort to establish or to improve Congressional relations and this indifference proved particularly surprising in light of the President's clear concern over his Party's weak numerical position. Where many GOP strategists urged co-operation and co-ordination the Administration

---

[26] Ford Timeline Documents, found at GRFPL, Vertical File.
[27] Brinkley, *Gerald R. Ford*, p. 35.
[28] DeGregorio, *The Complete Book of U.S. Presidents*, p. 609.
[29] Brinkley, *Gerald R. Ford*, p. 67.

saw the Republican Congressional delegation as enlisted foot soldiers, fit only to carry out orders given by superior officers. Nixon, a former member of Congress and a Senator who should have been cognizant of congressional sensibilities, often chose to ignore Congress altogether and simply imposed his will by the issuance of executive orders. The growing enmity between the executive and the legislative branch certainly handicapped the Nixon presidency during the first term. It proved fatal during the second term.

In 1970 Ford launched an odd campaign to impeach William O. Douglas, the liberal Justice of the U.S. Supreme Court. Some political historians speculate that the U.S. Senate rejection of Nixon Supreme Court nominees Clement Haynesworth and G. Harrold Carswell sparked this GOP retaliatory measure, with Ford leading the charge.[30] Regardless of the reasoning applied in the case, Minority Leader Ford cited Douglas for financial improprieties, especially for his ties to the Parvin Foundation, a charitable group with ties to organized crime, also for a tendency to live beyond his means, and for intemperate remarks that Douglas had uttered over the years. Ford charged that Douglas lacked the proper judicial temperament, and that the same standard applied to Supreme Court nominees should apply to jurists already on the bench. The cause failed to generate much momentum and died in committee. The affair brought Ford considerable criticism, however, from the Democrats and the prestige media. When pressed by skeptics on whether Douglas questionable behavior actually warranted impeachment, Ford insisted that an impeachable offense was anything that a majority of the House of Representatives determined at a given moment in time, and that a conviction required only that 2/3rds of the Senators considered the charges serious enough to warrant removal from office. Ford's own matter-of-fact approach to the possible impeachment of a high public official would come back to haunt him and his Party when opponents used a very similar argument against President Nixon during the coming years and the Watergate scandal.

---

[30] DeGregorio, The Complete Book of U.S. Presidents, p. 609.

Chapter 6

OUR LONG NATIONAL NIGHTMARE

As 1972 opened America faced another general election, and appeared to many observers an unsettled, and even a troubled country. The national economy slowed considerably during the previous year, signs of an inflationary cycle began to appear, and the American public witnessed a preview of the "stagflation" phenomenon that would plague the American economy for the next decade. The Nixon Administration abandoned traditional Republican free market dogma and employed a neo-Keynesian economic approach including increased government spending along with wage and price controls. Gerald Ford, leading the GOP Congressional delegation, swallowed his misgivings and publicly endorsed these policies.[1]

The country also faced the seemingly endless war in Southeast Asia. Nixon had campaigned for the Presidency in 1968 declaring that he had fashioned a secret plan to end the Vietnam War. As 1972 opened, the war still raged, albeit with far fewer American troops involved in the fighting than had been the case when Nixon took office in 1969. Nixon had, in fact, withdrawn large numbers of American combat troops, but had sanctioned a widening of the war, by authorizing American incursions into Laos and Cambodia, and by ordering the large scale bombing of North Vietnam. This overall policy aimed at breaking the North Vietnamese will to continue the fight, and while it ultimately succeeded, this was not apparent to the casual observer at the time.[2] The nation still seemed stuck in the Southeast Asian quagmire.

---

[1] Hayward, *The Age of Reagan,* pp. 264-268. Also see, Larry Schweikart and Michael Allen, A *Patriot's History of the United States,* (New York: Penguin Publishing, 2004) pp. 708-709.
[2] Schweikart and Allen, *A Patriot's History of the United States,* pp. 711-714.

America experienced little domestic tranquility as a result of these difficulties. College campus violence, a result of anti-war sentiment, began to wind down after 1970 but spontaneous demonstrations kept the nation on edge. While some commentators supported the general spirit of campus protests others lamented over what they regarded as a breakdown in public order and a decline in the standards of civic discourse and conduct. Indeed, a core electoral bloc, many of whom voted Republican for the first time in 1968, coalesced in the late 1960s and early 1970s. Nixon, himself, referred to them as "the silent majority" and actively sought their support. This constituency, largely working middle class in composition, deplored the perceived anti-Americanism of the protestors and the concomitant perceived slippage of American standing in the world. Historical hindsight indicates that this "slippage" may have been vastly overestimated, but many Americans of the 1970s vintage felt it very strongly, nonetheless.

American politics suffered from an identical sense of unsettledness in 1972. The mid-term elections of 1970 had turned out badly for the GOP. Gerald Ford saw his personal quest to win the House Speakership seriously set back when the Republicans lost twelve seats in the lower chamber. Given the national problems at the time, no credible observer expected a Republican takeover of the House in 1972. President Nixon's re-election appeared uncertain, as well.

As the primary election season opened some conservative Republicans expressed their support for Ronald Reagan, the former motion picture actor turned California governor, and GOP liberals continued their long love affair with Nelson Rockefeller, the former New York chief executive. Most highly placed Republican officials lined up behind the Nixon re-election effort. A group of dissatisfied Republicans engineered an effort to draft Ohio Congressman John Ashbrook, but this boomlet ran out of steam.[3] Nixon's incumbency and his corresponding control of the Party machinery guaranteed his renomination, but the fact that the President generated little enthusiasm within his own Party sounded an ominous note for the GOP in the near future.

The Democrats offered the real drama in the 1972 primary season. Veteran Democratic contenders like former Vice-President and current Minnesota Senator Hubert Humphrey, Washington Senator Henry J. "Scoop" Jackson, and Maine Senator Edmund Muskie all entered the race, but faltered early. George Wallace, the Alabama governor who had run surprisingly well for the Presidency on a third Party ticket in 1968, returned to the Democratic

---

[3] Edwards, The Conservative Revolution, pp. 172-174.

fold and ran well in the early primaries, but the Wallace campaign ground to a halt after a gunman shot and severely wounded the candidate in early May. At this point much of the Democratic attention shifted to a previously obscure South Dakota Senator named George McGovern. The young former B-24 bomber pilot won a Distinguished Flying Cross during World War II and later earned a doctoral degree in history. Large numbers of volunteers, most of them young college students and recent graduates, flocked to the McGovern campaign, eagerly imbibing the candidate's earnest liberalism. An older generation of Democrats showed much less fervor for the South Dakotan. Many seasoned Democratic political veterans sensed that a McGovern ticket might take the Party over a cliff in the general election, much like Goldwater had led the GOP to an Armageddon in 1964. Concerned Democrats pressed Senator Hubert Humphrey into the race as a last ditch effort to stop the McGovern bandwagon.[4]

The Humphrey challenge to McGovern's candidacy sputtered from the start and simply delayed, but did not prevent the South Dakota senator from clinching the Democratic nomination. McGovern's general election campaign was handicapped from the start by organizational weakness, poor staff work, and a lack of competence and talent. The campaign badly bungled the choice of a Vice-Presidential running mate, choosing Missouri Senator Thomas Eagleton, and then forcing the candidate off of the ticket less than three weeks later. The McGovernites eventually settled on a candidate whose only qualification for the Vice-Presidency was the fact that he had married into the Kennedy family! McGovern also proved to be a dull campaigner who had little flair for the glad-handing and backslapping of politics, and even less flair for public speaking. As the 1972 election approached many Democratic partisans privately conceded that their Party could not win.

The Republicans had, by the early spring, settled behind their President, Richard Nixon, albeit with little genuine passion. Nixon had pleased few of the natural GOP voting blocs during his term of office. Moreover, his secretive nature and the imperious attitude of his White House staff alienated key Republican figures on Capitol Hill, and in the country at large. Gerald Ford sensed this tension and vainly attempted to bridge the growing chasm between the President and his drifting Party.[5] On the morning of June 17, 1972 Ford was campaigning for the Republican Party and for himself in central

---

[4] Robert Novak, *The Prince of Darkness: 50 Years of Reporting In Washington*, (New York: Crown Publishing, 2007) pp. 224-227.

[5] Cannon, *Time And Chance*, pp. 98-99. Also see, Brinkley, *Gerald R. Ford*, pp. 43-46.

Michigan. He attended a county fair and, while driving to a local Chamber of Commerce event, he heard the startling news that five suspected political operatives had been arrested earlier that morning, caught in the act of burglarizing the Democratic National Committee headquarters, located in the Watergate office complex in Washington D.C. Ford later recalled that he was stunned by the sheer foolhardy and reckless nature of the deed and he believed that no seasoned political professionals could have been involved in such a harebrained scheme. Ford confronted the Nixon campaign chairman, John Mitchell, about the case and Mitchell denied any White House involvement in campaign skullduggery. Ford claimed that Mitchell's denial satisfied him that the White House had no part in the burgeoning outrage. The Watergate scandal, however, cast a long shadow, which would ultimately destroy the Nixon Presidency and would immeasurably affect the life and legacy of Gerald R. Ford, Jr.[6]

On November 7, 1972 Richard Nixon, leading the Republican ticket, rolled to a forty-nine state sweep of Senator George McGovern in the general election. The magnitude of the victory rivaled any landslide in American political history. Nixon broke the Democratic hold on the South, the large cities, the mountain states and the industrial Midwest, and even defeated McGovern in his home state of South Dakota. McGovern won only in Massachusetts and the District of Columbia.[7]

Yet, despite the Nixon juggernaut, a closer look shows that the 1972 election proved disappointing to Gerald Ford and his Republican legion. The GOP gained only twelve seats in the House of Representatives and actually lost two Senate seats. The Republicans would still face a fifty-seat deficit in the upcoming Congress. Furthermore, Nixon's own victory paled under closer examination. While he undoubtedly trounced McGovern, this victory came against a weak and inept opponent. Nearly half of the eligible voters stayed home in 1972, and the percentage turnout was the lowest since 1948.[8] A full 37% of the Democrats who bothered to go to the polls voted for Nixon, showing a remarkable lack of support for their own nominee. As Theodore White said, "It was not what the voters thought of Richard Nixon, but what they thought of George McGovern."[9]

---

[6] Ford, *A Time To Heal*, pp. 94-96.
[7] DeGregorio, *The Complete Book of U.S. Presidents*, p.610.
[8] Cannon, *Time And Chance*, p. 132.
[9] Theodore H. White, *The Making of the President 1972*, quoted in Cannon, *Time And Chance*, pp. 132-133.

Gerald Ford took the 1972 election as a bitter disappointment. His Party had once again claimed the Presidency, but Ford reluctantly conceded the likelihood that he would never become Speaker of the House of Representatives. Ford knew that he would lead his Party in a contentious political atmosphere, with many stormy battles ahead in 1973-74. He discussed his future with his wife Betty, and the family, and decided to remain House Minority Leader for two more years. He planned to run for re-election in 1974, relinquish his spot in the leadership, spend his final term as a backbencher, and retire from politics at the close of 1976.[10]

As the new Congress convened at the beginning of 1973, House Minority Leader Ford, like all other Congressional members watched the Watergate incident emerge as the overriding issue of the day. The Watergate scandal has been thoroughly essayed elsewhere and requires no long examination here. To recount briefly: In the very early morning of June 17, 1972 Washington D. C. police detectives arrested five men who were caught in the act of burglarizing the Democratic National Committee headquarters in the Watergate Hotel and Office complex in downtown Washington. The suspects were unarmed, but were carrying large amounts of cash in consecutively numbered one-hundred dollar bills, they were wearing rubber gloves, and appeared to be planting sophisticated listening devices in the offices. It soon came to light that these men were in the employ of the "Committee To Re-elect the President," (known thereafter as CREEP) an organization headed by former U.S. Attorney General John Mitchell, and operating out of the White House. President Nixon had no foreknowledge of the attempted burglary and was reportedly dumbfounded when he first heard reports of the arrest of minor campaign operatives in the action. Nixon, however, took no immediate action to address this misconduct. During the 1972 campaign the Democrats, understandably, sought to make Watergate an issue, but the American public seemed disinterested, believing, perhaps that the Parties routinely spied on each other. The issue lay dormant until early 1973.

Shortly after Nixon's second inauguration on January 20, 1973, the *Washington Post* and other major newspapers, and the television/radio media began directing fire at the Nixon Administration over the Watergate affair. The Senate voted on February 7, 1973 to hold public hearings on the matter with eighteen Republicans voting with the majority Democrats in favor of beginning a full inquiry. The Senate convened a special committee, called the "Senate Select Committee on Investigations," headed by Senator Sam Ervin of

---

[10] Brinkley, *Gerald R. Ford*, p. 49.

North Carolina and empowered the committee to conduct highly publicized hearings, which resulted in the steady release of damaging information concerning official misdeeds committed by members of the Nixon Administration. The President, in response to these disclosures, requested the resignations of several staff members and fired his personal White House counselor, John Dean. As the spring of 1973 gave way to summer certain Washington observers, mostly veteran journalists and professional politicos, began to whisper about the possibility of a Presidential impeachment. By August of 1973 the Watergate affair had cast a growing pall of gloom over the Nixon Administration.

Gerald Ford, good friend of Nixon and loyal Party man, publicly defended his boss. Ford seemed to ignore the issue, to the consternation of White House staffers, who seemed eager to enlist his help in sidetracking an investigation.[11] In his public comments Ford proved circumspect and correct. He spoke to constituents and GOP county committees in Michigan and defended the President, although he harbored growing suspicions about some of the White House staff and campaign aides.[12] Ford's greatest worry was that the Watergate cloud would ruin Republican chances of winning back Congress in the 1974 elections. He calculated, correctly, that the scandal was damaging the Party's standing and that public opinion was moving against the GOP. Ford could not easily distance the Party from President Nixon and, as a long time friend of Nixon, he refused to believe that the President could have been involved in such base activities. Ford stated publicly in the summer of 1973, "I have the greatest confidence in the President, and I am absolutely positive he had nothing to do with this mess."[13] Ford betrayed no sense of foreboding concerning White House culpability in the burgeoning scandal and he stoutly supported the President.

Ford's loyalty to the President soon brought rewards. On August 6, 1973 the news services reported that Vice-President Spiro Agnew was facing an official investigation for bribery, conspiracy, and tax evasion dating back to his days as Baltimore County Executive and later as the Maryland governor. Agnew boldly protested his innocence, but federal investigators in Baltimore amassed convincing evidence that Agnew had shaken down contractors as Baltimore County Executive beginning in 1966. He continued these activities as Maryland governor and, briefly, as Vice-President of the United States. In addition to this malfeasance, Agnew had failed to declare and pay taxes on this

---

11 Cannon, Time And Chance, p. 129.
12 Ibid. p. 130.
13 Cannon, Time And Chance, pp. 154-159.

"income." The federal authorities began an investigation of Agnew in February of 1973 and the Vice-President was facing a significant prison sentence if convicted of a crime.[14]

The Nixon Administration, having considered dumping Agnew from the Presidential ticket in 1972, made no effort to save him in 1973. Agnew, himself, seemed inclined to put up a fight rather than to surrender. His resolve, however, ebbed away in the face of strong evidence against him and the growing realization that the Administration would cut him loose in order to avoid further collateral political damage. On October 10, 1973 Agnew declined to contest the charges in court and paid a fine of $10,000. He also resigned the Vice-Presidency of the United States in exchange for a grant of immunity against further prosecution.[15]

President Nixon now faced a situation unique in American history. The Twenty-Fifth Amendment to the Constitution, ratified in 1967, gave Congress the authority to confirm the President's choice for the Vice-Presidency, if a vacancy occurred in the office. Nixon knew that the Congress would carefully scrutinize his choice for the Vice-Presidency and that no controversial nominee would be allowed to slip through the dragnet. Nixon began canvassing the Republican VIP's, asking their advice and suggestions in order to find a candidate as quickly as possible. Due to the sudden vacancy House Speaker Carl Albert, a Democrat from Oklahoma, stood directly behind Nixon in line of succession to the Presidency.[16] Nixon's solicitation of Republican leaders turned up some interesting findings. Conservative stalwart Barry Goldwater, the choice of many Midwest and Mountain State Republicans, declared he had no interest in the position and suggested George H.W. Bush, the Chairman of the Republican National Committee. Kansas Senator Bob Dole, eager to offend no Party faction, submitted the President a list of eight names, arranged in alphabetical order. Gradually, Nixon's staff narrowed the field to four contenders: California Governor Ronald Reagan, Treasury Secretary John B. Connally, Ex-New York Governor Nelson Rockefeller, and House Minority Leader Gerald R. Ford.

Each of the prospective candidates carried clear assets, but also studied liabilities. Reagan, completing the second term of a largely successful governorship of the nation's largest state, had built a national following in conservative circles. Rockefeller, now out of office, remained the liberal

---

[14] Brinkley, *Gerald R. Ford*, p. 50.
[15] Schweikart and Allen, *A Patriot's History of the United States*, p. 719.
[16] Brinkley, *Gerald R. Ford*, p. 51. Also see, Cannon, *Time And Chance*, pp. 204-205.

Republican champion. Liberals, however, disdained Reagan and GOP conservatives still resented Rockefeller bitterly. If Nixon had selected either man it would have possibly renewed intramural hostility such as the Party had not seen since 1964. Treasury Secretary Connally, Nixon's personal choice, possessed crossover appeal as a former Democratic Texas governor. The GOP regulars, however, retained suspicions regarding Connally and Democrats in Congress hated him because he had switched sides. The Congress sent clear signals that they would veto a Connally nomination. Gerald Ford, however, clearly met the "passable" standard. He had served capably in Congress for a quarter-century and had made remarkably few enemies along the way. Conservative Republicans noted Ford's center-right inclinations, while the more liberal faction found him a comfortable fit because of his long time friendship with Rockefeller and the Party's moderate Eastern establishment. The Nixon staffers, after careful calculations, knew that Congress would confirm a Ford nomination. They knew that they had found their man.[17]

Nixon's personal feelings colored his decision making process, in this instance. The President mistrusted Nelson Rockefeller and neither liked nor trusted Ronald Reagan. He resented Reagan's rapid ascent form motion picture and television star to California governor. Making the same mistake that many, including Presidents Gerald Ford and Jimmy Carter would repeat, Nixon dismissed the charismatic California governor as an intellectual lightweight and a flash-in-the-pan. Nixon had recently developed a friendship with Treasury Secretary Connally and insisted on considering the veteran Texan for the office, despite tepid Party support. Nixon's long friendship with Ford certainly influenced his decision, but the President's personal regard for Ford ran in tandem with a certain understated degree of disdain for Ford's skills and capabilities. It has been said that during the height of the Vice-Presidential selection process Nixon, whose removal from the Presidency was by no means assured in the fall of 1973, sitting in the Oval Office, leaned back from his desk, and remarked, "Can you imagine Jerry Ford sitting in this chair?"[18]

Despite Nixon's ambivalence toward Ford and possible concerns about his ability the White House staff understood the fact that they were facing a conundrum in the autumn of 1973. House Speaker Carl Albert exercised an essential veto power over the proceedings and warned against Reagan, Rockefeller, and Connally. While Ford emerged by process of elimination as

---

[17] Edwards, The Conservative Revolution, p. 180.
[18] Patterson, Grand Expectations, p. 776-777.

the leading contender many Washington insiders denied this reality. As the celebrated journalist Robert Novak wrote, "... At 60, Gerald Ford is simply not considered among the top tier of Republicans."[19] Novak and others fell back on the old perception of Ford as an intellectual mediocrity and a plodder lacking imagination and ideas, but Ford's supposed weaknesses actually helped his cause, in the longer run. His low-key demeanor bespoke his essential steadiness of character and his genuine "nice guy" persona had produced few enemies in either Party. Potential critics found little political ammunition to use against Ford, as his non-ideological moderate conservatism excited few, but alarmed no one. Nixon and his staff eventually came to understand the benefits of a Ford nomination.

On October 12, 1973 President Richard Nixon nominated House Minority Leader Gerald R. Ford as Vice-President of the United States. The President and his staff expected a quick confirmation, but the Congress, operating in an increasingly poisonous partisan atmosphere, held off on Ford's confirmation until December 6, 1973. The vote in the House of Representatives broke down 387-48 and in the Senate 92-3, with Senators Gaylord Nelson of Wisconsin, William Hathaway of Maine, and Thomas Eagleton of Missouri, all Democrats, voting to reject the Ford nomination. Gerald R. Ford took the oath of office as the Vice-President of the United States the following day.

During his abbreviated stint as the Vice-President, Ford found himself playing much the same role he had played as House Minority Leader. He barnstormed the country speaking on behalf of the Party, and its candidates, although in his new role he emphasized Presidential initiatives, rather than strictly legislative matters. Ford mistakenly assumed that his Vice-Presidential role would be that of a Capitol Hill figure, presiding over the Senate and lobbying for the Administration. He soon found that he would better serve the President by doing what he had grown accustomed to doing as a GOP Congressional leader, which was stumping the country and making the case for Administration positions.

During his eight months as the Vice-President, Ford logged 118,000 miles, and he made over 500 personal appearances in 40 states.[20] He spoke to any group that would engage him, at any time, and any place. In practice, Ford often found himself in second tier cities, speaking to solidly Republican assemblages, on matters within his realm of expertise. He concentrated on legislative affairs, foreign and defense policy, and the slumping state of the

---

[19] Novak, The Prince of Darkness, p. 253.
[20] Brinkley, Gerald R. Ford, p. 55.

economy. As journalist Richard Reeves opined, "Gerald Ford's America was a mind-blurring parade of middle-aged men in double-knit suits-- the small businessmen and corporate executives who are the core and soul of the Republican Party--holding plastic cups of Scotch at $25-a-couple receptions in the Windsor Room of motels outside medium sized cities."[21] As a general rule Ford tried to avoid Watergate as much as possible, although this became more difficult as time passed and the atmosphere of a nation in constitutional crisis deepened. When questioned on Watergate, Ford regularly professed his belief that Nixon was innocent of any wrongdoing.

Meanwhile, the Watergate shadow lengthened, and the consequences sometimes proved embarrassing for Vice-President Ford. In January of 1974, Ford offered a fiery defense of his boss in Atlantic City, while speaking to the American Farm Bureau federation. Longtime Ford associates blanched at the tone of the speech, noting that it ran counter to the Vice-President's non-combative nature. Journalistic spadework turned up the fact that White House speechwriter and noted conservative firebrand Patrick J. Buchanan actually wrote the address and Ford had given the speech without reading it in advance. The same day a team of audio experts who had been studying the infamous Oval Office tape recording system determined that the eighteen-minute gap in the recording of the June 20, 1972 meeting between President Nixon and Chief-of-Staff H.R. Haldeman had been created by five separate acts of erasure. These findings were released publicly a few hours after Ford addressed the Farm Bureau. Following this embarrassment Ford tamped down his rhetoric, but he did not abandon his defense of Nixon.

Still, a close study of Ford's actions during his Vice-Presidency shows a subtle change in his rhetoric as the Watergate affair mushroomed. Ford sought to avoid the subject while barnstorming the country, yet he found that his audiences would ask questions about nothing else. As the winter of 1974 gave way to spring Ford moderated his rhetoric to include a caveat, saying that he had seen no evidence to indicate that the President had committed a crime. He continued to repeat this mantra into the summer as the Administration's troubles deepened. Ford did not want to be seen as disloyal to his boss, nor was he seeking the presidency for himself. Interestingly, he declined Nixon's offer to allow him to listen to the tapes that the President had refused to surrender to investigators. Ford assured Nixon that he took the President at his

---

[21] Richard Reeves, *A Ford Not A Lincoln,* (New York: Harcourt, Brace & Jovanovich, 1975) pp. 46-49.

word and, more importantly, his refusal to examine evidence preserved the plausibility of his statement concerning the evidence he had seen.

While Ford played the role of Nixon loyalist in public, he privately questioned his old mentor's actions. Ford had, in fact, argued that Nixon should surrender the requested materials to federal investigators, thereby closing the matter for good. Nixon's refusal to do so, on the grounds of executive privilege, struck Ford as stubborn and obtuse. Ford actually began to suspect that the White House was withholding incriminating evidence and was playing him for a fool, by sending him out to publicly defend the Administration. In addition, Ford found that Nixon seemed to care little about the anti-Republican tsunami building across the country.[22] All signs pointed to a GOP rout in the coming November 1974 midterm elections. The Democrats had even won Ford's old House seat in a February 1974 special election, the first time since 1910 that a Republican candidate lost the Fifth Congressional District in Michigan. Clearly, Nixon was sinking and pulling the Party down with him. Ford, ever the Republican stalwart, found his old friend's indifference to the Party an outrage.

In March of 1974 the President faced a nearly open rebellion in his own Party when New York Senator James Buckley, a leading conservative and brother of *National Review* publisher William F. Buckley, proposed that Nixon resign for the good of the country. Buckley undoubtedly considered the good of the GOP in his calculations, as well. He realized, as did many of his colleagues, that the Party would suffer a ruinous defeat in the fall election and that Nixon was providing a lightning rod for the anti-GOP sentiment. Buckley's proposal failed to generate much open support. Privately, though, the Republican legislative contingent began to circle the wagons in the face of mounting evidence that the President was more involved in Watergate than he had led them to believe.

Public opinion was now turning sharply against the Administration, as its troubles deepened. In February, the full House of Representatives authorized the Judiciary Committee to begin an impeachment investigation by the startling vote of 410-4. This lopsided margin shocked the Nixon team and finally convinced them of the serious nature of their predicament. Meanwhile, the Nixon legal defense team sparred with investigators, the Special Prosecutors office, judges, and the Congress concerning the Oval Office tapes. In April, Nixon released White House-edited tapes of forty-six private conversations. The President acknowledged that the contents of the tapes

---

[22] Edwards, The Conservative Revolution, pp. 180-181.

would prove personally embarrassing, but would also confirm the lack of criminal culpability of the Chief Executive and his staff. Nixon also announced that he would obey a definitive ruling from the U.S. Supreme Court concerning the release of the contested audiotapes. The Supreme Court duly issued such a ruling on July 24, 1974 in the case of *U.S. v. Nixon*, when the court unanimously stated that a presidential claim of executive privilege could not be invoked to withhold evidence required in a criminal investigation. The Administration reluctantly surrendered another sixty-four tapes.

Back on the political front, the House Judiciary Committee approved three articles of impeachment against President Nixon on July 28th. The committee declared that Nixon had violated his oath of office by obstructing justice in the Watergate cover-up, abusing his power through the illegal use of the Internal Revenue Service, Federal Bureau of Investigation, the Central Intelligence Agency, the Secret Service, and the Department of Justice to harass private citizens, and for contempt of Congress in refusing to comply with congressional subpoenas and non-cooperation in the Watergate investigation. Six Republican committee members joined all twenty-one Democrats in approving the first article and seven Republicans joined all of the Democrats in approving the second article of impeachment.[23]

The House of Representatives set a date of August 19, 1974 to begin debate on the measures to impeach President Nixon. After consulting with allies, the President believed that he could win an impeachment fight, but any possibility that he could remain in office (which would have been slim, at best) vanished on August 5, 1974 with the release of the so-called "smoking gun" taped conversations, in which Nixon and his Chief-of-Staff H.R. Haldeman clearly directed subordinates to derail a Watergate investigation by any means necessary, including using federal agencies to obstruct justice, conducting official harassment of Nixon's "enemies," and paying hush money to ensure the silence of those who could give evidence against the Administration. Nixon's removal from office was now a certainty.[24]

When did Vice-President Gerald Ford realize that he would soon become the President of the United States? No historical consensus exists on this question. Thomas DeFrank, a veteran journalist who served as the *Newsweek* correspondent covering Ford during the Vice-Presidential interlude, insists that Ford grasped the reality of the situation as early as April of 1974. Certainly Ford, a student of the Constitution as well as a practical politician, understood

---

[23] Patterson, *Grand Expectations*, pp. 773-778.
[24] Ibid. 773-780.

that he might become the President at any time. The Nixon White House had chosen him carefully for the second spot precisely because of the fact that the new Vice-President would be stepping aboard a listing vessel, if not yet a sinking ship. Nixon's slowly eroding support was clear by late 1973, but his position was not yet desperate. The crisis atmosphere that seemed to envelop the Administration in 1974 showed the change in Ford's thinking concerning the likelihood of Nixon remaining in office.[25]

In Thomas DeFrank's memoir entitled, *Write It When I'm Gone*, the author claims that he had a private conversation with Ford, in which the Vice-President acknowledged the probability that he would soon be the President of the United States. "… Now impulsively he had blurted out the truth. Four months before it actually happened, three months before the Supreme Court ordered Nixon to turn over the tape recordings that would doom him, Ford had just admitted he knew in his gut that Nixon was a goner and he would soon become America's 38th, and first unelected president."[26]

The release of the "smoking gun" tape transcripts sealed Nixon's fate. The President could not easily decide on whether he would resign or stay on to fight a losing impeachment battle. On August 1, 1974 Nixon's Chief-of-Staff Alexander Haig advised Ford to prepare for a transition to the Presidency. Haig questioned Ford on the possibility of a pardon for Nixon, but Ford refused to commit himself to any specific course of action.[27] While rumors swirled around Washington regarding Nixon's future during the summer of 1974 Vice-President Ford took a first step toward jumping ship. Ford attended a cabinet meeting on Tuesday morning, August 6th, and told Nixon that he would continue to support Administration policies and initiatives, but he refused to continue a public defense of the President on the Watergate affair.[28]

On Thursday, August 8, 1974 Ford met with Nixon in the Oval Office at 11:00 AM. The President, showing the strain of the recent months, appeared exhausted and worn.[29] Nixon informed Ford of his intention to resign and said, "… I know you'll do well."[30] The two men spent the next hour reminiscing about their quarter-century together in national politics. Ford claimed that he experienced no joy in claiming the Presidency, only sadness in the ruination of

---

[25] Thomas DeFrank, Write It When I'm Gone: Remarkable Off-The-Record Conversations With Gerald R. Ford, (New York: Penguin Publishing, 2007) pp. 35-40.
[26] Ibid. p. 14.
[27] Ford Timeline Documents, Found at GRFPL, Vertical File.
[28] Brinkley, Gerald R. Ford, p. 62.
[29] Ibid. pp. 62-63.
[30] Ford Timeline Documents, Found at GRFPL, Vertical File.

an old friend. That evening Nixon, in a televised address to the nation, announced he would resign the Presidency and that Vice-President Ford would take the oath of office at noon, the following day.

On Friday morning, August 9, 1974 President Nixon submitted his formal resignation to the Secretary of State and flew off to his home at San Clemente, California, now a private citizen. At 12:03 PM Warren Burger, Chief Justice of the Supreme Court, swore in Gerald R. Ford, Jr. as the Thirty-Eighth President of the United States. Ford, as would become habitual later on, delivered a short and dry address to the nation. It became memorable only for the opening line: "My fellow Americans, our long national nightmare is over."[31]

---

[31] Brinkley, *Gerald R. Ford*, p. 31.

Chapter 7

MR. PRESIDENT

Gerald Ford offered an immediate clue as to the work habits he would establish as the President of the United States. Following his swearing in ceremony he went to work directly, meeting with the White House staff, his transition advisers, a congressional delegation, and several foreign ambassadors. He then convened a meeting of his Council of Economic Advisers. Ford showed early on that he would follow the same routine that he had practiced in Congress wherein he rose early, exercised, and began a long day of work before 7:00 AM. He would stick to this regimen throughout his Presidency.[1]

On August 12, 1974 Ford addressed a joint session of Congress. Mindful of his relatively fragile political position and the problems Nixon had created by ignoring the Congress, Ford set an agreeable tone. He stated, "... I do not want a honeymoon with you. I want a good marriage." He avoided a deep policy analysis in his address, except to say that the nation had to bring currency inflation under control, declaring it to be "Public Enemy Number One." The effect of Ford's speech was startling, and for the President and his Party, very happily so. Official Washington, and the nation as a whole, breathed a sigh of relief at closing of the Watergate melodrama, and Ford, himself, offered a welcome contrast to "Tricky Dick" Nixon. Ford's open nature, low key demeanor, and his reputation for honesty and integrity reassured a nation wearied of Machiavellian intrigue, imperial presidencies, and wrongdoing in high places. Moreover, the Ford family, now living in the White House, seemed the very picture of normality. The President, the First

---

[1] Ford Timeline Documents, Found at GRFPL, Vertical File.

Lady, and their young adult children appeared to offer a throwback to the seemingly bygone days of the happy nuclear family, circa 1955. Ford enjoyed these happy moments but political realities would soon intrude upon this idyll.[2]

On August 20, 1974 Ford nominated Nelson Rockefeller, the ex-New York governor and quintessential liberal Republican, to serve as his Vice-President. The choice infuriated the conservatives in the GOP, just as many observers had predicted. Conservative Republicans bitterly remembered the Rockefeller-Goldwater tilt in 1964, and they never forgave the New Yorker for singling them out for scorn and ridicule at the San Francisco convention that summer. Rockefeller, for his own part, sensed the conservatives' antipathy and returned it with great relish.

The Rockefeller nomination emerged as the first major decision of the Ford Administration. Why did the new President select someone who would undoubtedly provoke a sizable segment of the Party? Why, if Rockefeller had been considered too "controversial" to be nominated for the Vice-Presidency in 1973, had he suddenly become acceptable a mere ten months later? Upon taking office, Ford had quietly conducted an impromptu poll of Republican leaders for a Vice-Presidential suggestion, and the leading candidate was George H.W. Bush, the Republican National Committee Chairman. James Baker and other Bush allies openly lobbied the White House on behalf of their man. Many Party leaders, however, considered Bush insufficiently experienced to step into the Vice-Presidency, while others considered him intellectually shallow.[3]

Ronald Reagan, also passed over for being "too controversial" in 1973 carried on a quiet but determined effort to land the nomination. Reagan's supporters argued that Ford's choice should be someone with proven executive experience (i.e., a California governor) and someone who supported the ideological mandate of the 1972 election, which meant a conservative like Reagan, not the liberal Rockefeller. Various State Republican organizations sent messages to Ford on Reagan's behalf and prominent private citizens like Reagan's old Hollywood friend and fellow actor John Wayne urged the President to nominate Reagan for the Vice-Presidency. Ford refused and tried to mollify Reagan by offering him two minor cabinet positions, and later on the ambassadorship to Great Britain. Reagan considered these offers insulting

---

[2] Brinkley, *Gerald R. Ford*, pp. 67-68. Also see Cannon, *Time And Chance*, pp. 350-360.
[3] Hayward, *The Age of Reagan*, p. 397.

and refused the positions. He also developed a grudge against the President, which would play a fateful role in 1976 and beyond.[4]

Ultimately, Ford chose Nelson Rockefeller, although no historical consensus exists as to why he chose the successor to one of the nation's most storied fortunes. White House aide Patrick J. Buchanan, later a conservative titan of renown, suggested that Reagan would ignite a firestorm of media abuse, while Rockefeller would command universal media approval. Historian Douglas Brinkley asserts that Ford chose Rockefeller for his name and his appeal. "... Rocky had star quality and Ford's PR instincts told him that was what his new Administration needed most."[5] Former journalist and Ford adviser James Cannon dismissed this breathless and dramatic explanation, and simply stated that Ford wanted a steady and proven leader in the second spot. Regardless of motive, Ford offered Rockefeller the Vice-Presidency on August 17, 1974. The former New York governor accepted the offer the following day and the White House formally announced the Rockefeller nomination on August 20th.

The Republican conservatives immediately slammed the nomination, which they considered a slap-in-the-face. The Administration expected a conservative backlash and dismissed it, saying that it was important to find a candidate who would win easy congressional confirmation. Administration functionaries assumed that Rockefeller would win easy confirmation, but they were wrong. The Democrats subjected Rockefeller to a very tough grilling, mostly on the subject of his complex financial affairs, and his total wealth estimated at $218 million (1974) dollars. After a long and contentious confirmation process Rockefeller gained congressional approval and took the oath as the Vice-President in December of 1974.[6]

The Ford Administration brought a firestorm of criticism down on its own head when nominating Rockefeller, but this served as a mere warm-up for the fury Ford unleashed on September 8, 1974. On that Sunday morning President Ford granted a "full, free and absolute pardon" to former President Nixon "for all offenses against the United States which he ... has committed, or may have committed, or taken part in" during his term in office.[7] The President, in a nationally televised address, declared that a long period of delay and the protracted litigation pursuant to a legal action would paralyze the government,

---

[4] Ibid. p. 398.
[5] Brinkley, *Gerald R. Ford*, p. 66.
[6] DeGregorio, *The Complete Book of U.S. Presidents*, p. 610.
[7] Ibid. p. 612.

inflame partisan passions, and bring into question the credibility of the national institutions. Ford later claimed that his White House staff assistants spent 90% of their time answering legal requests for documents and otherwise working on Nixon-related tasks. He calculated that his team could never function properly as long as the legal specter of a Nixon prosecution hung over the country. He moved quickly to exorcise this ghost.[8]

A careful analysis of Ford's statements and actions seems to confirm this truth. Ford realized that his Administration could not establish itself, and advance a legislative agenda while it devoted the majority of its time to matters involving Nixon and his alleged misdeeds. He wanted to put the matter behind the country and to start over with the Congress, in the hopes of successfully confronting the national problems. Ford undoubtedly felt a natural sympathy for his old friend and colleague Richard Nixon. Nixon had fallen ill with phlebitis and the reports out of San Clemente concerning his health, both physical and mental, were not encouraging. Ford issued the pardon because he believed it served the nation and because it aroused his own humane instincts. Ford expected controversy as a result of the pardon and he found his judgment correct.

The Nixon pardon immediately drew a storm of impassioned criticism. Ford's own press secretary Jerald F. TerHorst resigned in protest. Most of Ford's Republican colleagues muted their disapproval, except for conservative stalwart Senator Barry Goldwater, who publicly disparaged the President's action. Democrats, predictably, railed against the pardon and the president, some publicly hinting at the possibility of a "second impeachment."[9] The fire directed at the White House originated from all quarters, not only from rival politicians. The press denounced the pardon in editorials and commentary nationwide. The public reaction was universally negative and the President's standing dropped over twenty points in most public opinion polls. Ford had seemed to many people a refreshing change in tone and style from the Nixon Administration, but after the pardon he came to represent simple politics as usual in Washington. Influential persons voiced suspicions that Ford and Nixon had "made a deal," in effect trading the presidency for a pardon. This supposition spread widely in the following weeks.

At the stroke of a pen, Ford squandered the public goodwill and the reputation for integrity and rectitude he had cultivated over a quarter-century in public life. The *New York Times, Washington Post,* and other organs of the

---

[8] Ford, *A Time To Heal*, pp. 159-181.
[9] Hayward, *The Age of Reagan*, p. 397.

prestige media claimed that the pardon reeked of suspicion, that Ford now engaged in the same type of abuses of power as Nixon, and that the new President could no longer be taken at his word. The Nixon pardon damaged Ford's reputation badly and it did irreparable harm to his Presidency. The unanswered question remains the same now as it emerged then: Why?[10]

A full analysis of the pardon issue and Ford's reasoning in granting one indicates a number of motivations. Certainly, Ford may be taken at his word when he suggested that 90% of his own time, as well as that of his Administration, would be dominated by Nixon-related labors. Ford found, to his dismay, that half of the questions at his first press conference dealt with Nixon and the possibility of a Presidential pardon.[11] Secondly, Ford sincerely hoped to put the issue to rest in order to pursue a positive legislative agenda. In a private conversation with Henry Kissinger, whom Ford had retained as his Secretary of State, Ford remarked, "Henry we've got to put this behind us, and get on with all the other things we have to do."[12] Finally, Ford showed a great deal of loyalty to an old personal friend and colleague, as he was truly saddened by Nixon's plight. The ex-President resided at his California home in a state of genteel disgrace. Rumors had begun to circulate concerning the ex-President's precarious physical and mental health, and he would suffer a number of maladies requiring hospitalization in the coming months. Ford simply rejected the idea of furthering Nixon's ignominy by subjecting him to a full criminal trial in a federal court. In response to arguments that Nixon deserved censure and punishment for alleged misdeeds, Ford answered that the ex-President had paid a full price, in view of the crash of his public career and his ruined reputation.

Questions linger today on whether Ford agreed to a deal in the Nixon pardon matter. The historical consensus suggests that the involved parties made no deal to pardon Nixon. Ford had refused to address this matter in a conversation with Nixon's Chief-Of-Staff, Alexander Haig, shortly before Nixon's resignation in early August. It is highly unlikely that Ford would have summarily refused a pardon for Nixon and reversed course by granting the pardon one month later. Ford's noted honesty and integrity would never have permitted an unseemly deal whereby he took the Presidency and issued Nixon a pardon in return. Regardless of such a certainty, the Ford Administration sustained virtually permanent damage as a result of the Nixon pardon.

---

[10] Brinkley, *Gerald R. Ford*, pp. 67-73. Also see Cannon, *Time And Chance*, pp. 378-385.
[11] Ibid.
[12] DeGregorio, *The Complete Book of U.S. Presidents*, pp. 610-612.

Ford's gesture, ostensibly undertaken to help heal the nation, actually ginned up bitterness and hostility. The Democrats demanded answers to their questions and Ford agreed to personally testify before the House Judiciary Committee on October 17, 1974. Ford's appearance, although quite historical in nature, in fact shed no light on the issue. Ford did admit that he had discussed the possibility of a pardon with Al Haig but, under harsh questioning from committee members he thundered back at them, "There was no deal, period."[13]

The Nixon pardon would prove an albatross for the Ford Administration. The President showed his political ineptitude in issuing the controversial get-out-of-jail-free card to Nixon a mere two months before the 1974 mid-term elections. Public opinion, already trending anti-Republican, turned sharply against the GOP in the fall of 1974. In the November election the Democrats won five seats in the Senate and over forty in the House of Representatives.[14] The Republican congressional numbers fell to their lowest total since 1936. Ford had placed a great deal of emphasis on the elections as a measure of public confidence in his stewardship and the voters had responded by electing a nearly veto-proof Democratic majority. Clearly, in both chambers of the legislature, the President would find trouble ahead in 1975-76.

From the outset of his term Ford faced an ominous political environment in Washington. The Watergate scandal and the crisis that followed had created a toxic political atmosphere. In addition, the domestic economy, showing signs of weakness since the early 1970s fell into a severe slump in 1974. Unemployment increased and inflation, as measured by consumer prices, approached the double-digit level. The Arab oil embargo of late 1973 hiked energy prices considerably and the ripple effect spread to the larger economy during the winter and spring of 1974. Ford believed that the government could contain both inflation and recession-related unemployment by cutting government spending, balancing the federal budget, deregulating key industries, and decontrolling energy prices to stimulate production. He believed that these steps, woven together into a coherent program, would overcome the energy shortage and contain the startling growth in the size and cost of the federal government. As Ford often said, "A government big enough to give us everything we want is a government big enough to take away from us everything we have." The Democrats in Congress disagreed with Ford and he used his veto power 68 times in confrontations over government

---

[13] Brinkley, *Gerald R. Ford*, p. 74.
[14] Ibid.

spending.[15] The Democrats were able to override Ford's veto on occasion, but he usually prevailed. Ford also showed flexibility and willingness to compromise, which led to the approval of bills involving energy decontrol, tax reform, airline and railroad regulation, securities reform and an overhaul of anti-trust laws.[16]

Ford and his economic advisers decided that inflation presented the most pressing economic threat, and chose to tackle this problem first. On October 8, 1974 Ford unveiled his inflation-fighting program in a speech to a joint session of Congress. He proposed to substantially reduce government spending and urged the Congress to adopt a 5 % surcharge on individual and corporate taxes, as a means of balancing the federal budget. He labeled this program the "WIN" campaign, (with WIN standing as an acronym for "Whip Inflation Now") wore a lapel button, and suggested that the public join in the effort by purchasing and wearing their own WIN buttons. (Inexplicably, 100,000 people did!) This proposal provided late night comedians a rich vein for jokes and, more importantly, it seemed to suggest that Ford lacked the intellectual gravity to confront a serious issue in a substantive manner. The Administration gradually retired the WIN program, lapel-buttons and all, as the 1974-75 recession deepened. Ford, himself, later admitted that the WIN campaign was "probably too gimmicky."[17]

The Administration tinkered with laws to provide equity in the marketplace and to help consumers make informed decisions by pushing four bills through Congress in 1975. The Fair Credit Billing Act, The Real Estate Settlement Procedure Act, the Equal Credit Opportunity Act, and the Magnuson-Moss Warranty Act aimed to provide "equity in the marketplace." In a 1975 effort to curb oil consumption Ford imposed a duty on imported oil and signed into law a bill to initiate, over a period of 40 months, the complete decontrol of domestic oil prices.[18]

The Democrats in Congress grimly fought Ford over his fiscal and tax policies. While domestic political considerations doubtlessly influenced much of the opposition, the Democrats criticized Ford's single-minded devotion to curbing inflation. They suggested a combination of increased government spending (on welfare and public works) and a tax cut, which they assumed would be popular in the country, at large. Ford, like many conservatives,

---

[15] Ford Timeline Documents, Found at GRFPL, Vertical File.
[16] Ibid.
[17] Ford, *A Time To Heal,* p. 204.
[18] DeGregorio, *The Complete Book of U.S. Presidents,* p. 613.

enunciating the popular orthodoxy of the times, opposed a tax cut, and argued in favor of keeping a lid on the growth of government spending.

The Democratic tax-cutting proposal proved appealing to most of the political class, just as the Party leaders had expected. Ford, over the objections of his Treasury Secretary William Simon, proposed his own tax cut in the State-of-the-Union message in early 1975. Ford's economic team, led by Council of Economic Advisers Alan Greenspan, argued that a modest tax reduction would not increase the budget deficit because the added economic "kick-start" from the tax cut would bring in higher revenues due to increased economic activity. Although no one realized it at the time, the Republicans were taking the first steps toward a new conservative orthodoxy, one that became central to Reaganite thinking in the 1980s and beyond.[19]

The Democrats refused to cede the field to the GOP on the fiscal issue and promptly upped the ante. They proposed a larger tax cut than Ford requested and rejected all of the proposed spending cuts, which threatened to balloon the deficit to $100 billion. Ford threatened to use his veto but realized that the Congress would vote to override. The President grudgingly accepted the Democrats' proposed tax cut bill of $28 billion (over one year) in March of 1975. Still, the precarious state of the economy would remain a cloud on the horizon during Ford's entire term of office, and would contribute to his electoral defeat in 1976.[20]

Ford took his strongest stand against extravagant spending in the fall of 1975, in response to the developing financial crisis in New York City. The national metropolis had consistently spent beyond its means with city expenditures having risen by 12% annually since 1965, while revenues grew by only 5% during the same period. The city budget had trebled in one decade. The chickens came home to roost in the spring of 1975 when the city ran out of both cash and credit. New York City Mayor Abe Beame and the state Governor Hugh Carey personally visited the White House and proposed that Ford should design a federal "bail-out" for New York City by endorsing loan guarantees in the form of a billion dollars in municipal bonds. Ford and his economic advisers, led by Treasury Secretary William Simon, himself a former Wall Street investment banker, rejected the entreaties and placed the blame for the crisis squarely on the city, itself, for creating the conditions that led to the financial insolvency.

---

[19] Hayward, *The Age of Reagan*, pp. 400-401
[20] Schweikart and Allen, *A Patriot's History of the United States*, pp. 727-731. Also see Brinkley, *Gerald R. Ford*, pp. 83-85.

On October 29, 1975 Ford publicly refused Federal aid to New York City. Citing the imperative of fiscal restraint, he proposed that the city submit to a formal bankruptcy declaration in order to ensure a legally supervised default process. Ford and his team believed that New York officials lacked the will to make difficult decisions that would solve municipal problems. Throwing more money at the problems would only exacerbate them. Ford lectured the New York City leaders on the necessity of implementing sound budget policies and limiting unnecessary city services. Ford's speech, delivered at the National Press Club, prompted the *New York Daily News* to headline their lead editions the following morning in a seventy-two point bold type, "Ford To City: Drop Dead."

Ford understood that by holding to his hard line on a New York City bailout he was essentially forfeiting the huge New York electoral vote in the upcoming 1976 election, but he stuck to his guns. Ford and his economic advisers including Treasury Secretary Simon, Council of Economic Advisers Chair Greenspan, and Federal Reserve Chairman Arthur Burns did not rule out future aid to New York, but insisted that the city must seriously confront the root of their problems. Ford recalled in his memoir that New York City officials had no strategy for addressing their problems. "Beame and Carey had no answers. Nor did they have a plan ... and their demands were ridiculous."[21]

In November of 1975 the New York municipal and state administrations announced an austerity program, which would combine tax increases and reduced expenditures as a step toward solving their problems. Ford, encouraged by this supposed newfound resolve, reversed his field. On November 26, 1975 he endorsed legislation giving New York access to $2.3 billion in direct loans in each of the next three fiscal years. The Congress complied with Ford's request and he signed the bill on December 9, 1975.

The fallout from the New York City situation began immediately. Ford, indeed, alienated large electoral blocs in both New York City and the State, especially the police officers and firemen who lost their jobs. They would turn out in large numbers to vote Democratic in 1976. The heartland, meanwhile, took a dim view of the somewhat mislabeled "bailout," seeing it as an unholy alliance of big government and the American urban metropolis. The fact that Ford backed the bailout four weeks after strongly denouncing the possibility reinforced his image, in the minds of many, as a waffler and a bungler.[22]

---

[21] Ford, *A Time To Heal*, p. 316.
[22] Brinkley, *Gerald R. Ford*, p. 128.

Events taking place in 1975 served to remind the people and the President that 1960s style bitterness still lingered in the land. During the year two FBI Agents were killed in a standoff at the Pine Ridge Indian Reservation in South Dakota. Also the Weather Underground bombed the U. S. State Department in Washington and, late in the year, a bomb detonated at LaGuardia Airport in New York killed eleven people. In July, the Teamsters Union President, Jimmy Hoffa, disappeared, presumed to have been kidnapped and killed.[23] This spate of apparently 1960s style turmoil really hit the country in September of 1975 when assassins twice attempted to murder President Ford while he visited California.

On September 5, 1975 the President paid an official visit to the California state capital at Sacramento, to confer with the newly elected Governor, Jerry Brown, and ironically to address the California state legislature on crime! Before the scheduled gubernatorial meeting the President "met the people," and shook hands with the crowd outside of the California state capitol building. A twenty-six year old woman, Lynette "Squeaky" Fromme, later revealed to have been a follower of the deranged murderer Charles Manson, positioned herself two feet away form the President, calmly drew a .45 caliber pistol from a thigh holster, and pointed it directly at President Ford. She actually squeezed the trigger, but the gun failed to fire because there was no cartridge in the chamber, although the weapon did contain an ammunition clip. Secret Service Agents quickly wrestled Miss Fromme to the ground.

Gerald Ford, steady and unflappable as ever, calmly proceeded to his meeting with Governor Brown. He made no mention of the incident and simply discussed his economic policy with the California governor. Donald Rumsfeld, Ford's Chief-of-Staff, briefly interrupted the meetings to forward the President a preliminary report on the attempted assassination. The President then addressed the state legislature, just as previously planned. Ford certainly earned great public credit for grace under fire!

A mere seventeen days later, on September 22, 1975, Sara Jane Moore, a left-wing political activist who had served as an FBI informant, attempted to assassinate Ford in San Francisco. Ford had concluded the last event of the West Coast tour, which had been a local television interview at the St. Francis Hotel. Ford walked out of the hotel lobby and headed for the Presidential limousine. Sara Jane Moore drew a .38 caliber revolver from her handbag and fired one shot at the President from a distance of approximately forty feet. An alert bystander slapped at Moore's arm, knocking her slightly off balance. The

---

[23] Ibid. p. 120.

shot missed Ford by a few feet, ricocheted off of a curb, and hit a taxi driver, but did only superficial damage. Secret Service men pounced on the President and pushed him into the waiting limo, which sped away. Ford, once again undaunted, simply remarked, "Can we turn on the air conditioner? It's getting rather stuffy in here."[24] President Ford handled the two attempts on his life in his characteristically understated fashion. He accepted this as an unappetizing occupational hazard, and made it clear that it would have no bearing on his future public appearances. Ford, did, however, begin wearing a bulletproof vest underneath his suits during public appearances, at the insistence of his Secret Service detail.

A sure sign that Ford lead the nation during changing times was the non-traditional role played by his wife, the nation's First Lady. Betty Ford approached her role as the First Lady with the openness and genial good nature that would soon become her mark in trade. She held her first press conference on September 4, 1974, facing 75 reporters.[25] She took questions and frankly discussed controversial topics such as legalized abortion and the proposed Equal Rights Amendment. During her tenure as First Lady she became an outspoken advocate for women's rights during a time of extensive public debate on the matter, and the nature of "equal rights." She encouraged the appointment of more women to senior government positions and she addressed the International Women's Year meeting in 1975.

On August 10, 1975 Betty appeared on the CBS News program "60 Minutes." She shocked some viewers by admitting to CBS newsman Morley Safer that she might have tried marijuana if she had been young in the 1970s and she praised the Supreme Court's decision in legalizing abortion in *Roe v. Wade* (calling it a "great, great decision").[26] She also said that she wouldn't be surprised if her 18 year old daughter engaged in premarital sexual intercourse. While Mrs. Ford's candor pleased some it shocked others. The political and cultural right wing denounced the First Lady vociferously. James Burnham, writing in *National Review* expressed the feelings of a segment of the population when he criticized the President for "having a wife who won't keep her mouth shut."[27] The editors of the same magazine declared jokingly, "Mrs. Ford ought to know it is not up to her to rewrite the Ten Commandments on

---

[24] Ford, *A Time To Heal*, pp. 309-312.
[25] Betty Ford Timeline Documents, Found at GRFPL, Vertical File.
[26] Ibid.
[27] "Betty Ford Gaffe," *National Review*, August 29, 1975, p. 922.

nationwide TV."[28] The White House mail ran over two-to-one in opposition to Mrs. Ford's remarks but within a month of her television interviews her public approval ratings climbed to nearly 75%.

Betty's husband would have liked to claim some of that popularity for himself. The ominous rumblings of political thunder vibrated across the nation in 1975. Conservative Republicans, never fully comfortable with Ford, looked westward to Los Angeles, and found their champion in Ronald Reagan, the ex-film and television star turned governor of California. Reagan had served two largely successful terms as the chief executive of the Golden State, and he now emerged as a vocal critic of a President from his own Party. Reagan, and the conservative Republicans in general, turned most of their fire on Ford's conduct of foreign policy.

When Ford took over the Presidency certain individuals within the Foreign Affairs-Defense-Intelligence troika expressed concern about the new man's "readiness" to conduct the national foreign policy. Ford knew of this uncertainty and bristled at these suspicions. He pointedly rejected the consensus opinion that he was a novice in foreign and defense policy, informing the skeptics that he grasped both the shaping and the conduct of foreign policy very well from his days on the House Defense Appropriations Committee and the Intelligence Subcommittee. Critics countered that Ford's supposed conduct of foreign policy consisted principally in opposing the JFK-LBJ Democratic initiatives, due to the fact that the Republicans, as the minority Party, could not muster the necessary numbers to unveil any substantial proposals of their own.

While Ford may have resented jabs at his foreign policy credentials, he partially conceded the point when he largely retained the foreign policy team he had inherited from the Nixon Administration.[29] Ford told Nixon that he would keep Secretary of State Henry Kissinger in his position, and he kept this promise, to the chagrin of many Republican conservatives. Ford did reduce Kissinger's duties by naming Air Force General Brent Scowcroft as his National Security Adviser. Later in his term Ford made a number of changes by naming his first Chief-Of-Staff Donald Rumsfeld as the new Defense Secretary and naming George H.W. Bush as the new Director of Central Intelligence, replacing William Colby. Mostly though, Ford initiated few major changes. As Ford biographer James Cannon wrote, "In conducting

---

[28] Ibid.
[29] Ford Timeline Documents, Found at GRFPL, Vertical File.

foreign affairs Ford was committed to continuity, he fully supported Nixon's policies, and kept Nixon's people."[30]

The most important of Nixon's people Ford retained in office was Henry Kissinger, the Secretary of State. Kissinger had been born in Furth, Germany and immigrated to the United States in 1938 as Nazi persecution of German Jews intensified. Kissinger served in the U.S. Army during World War II and later earned undergraduate and doctoral degrees from Harvard. In 1957 Kissinger attracted national attention when he published a book entitled, *Nuclear Weapons and Foreign Policy*. He advocated the idea of seeking peace through a general balance of power; an idea that critics charged amounted to coming to terms with formerly adversarial governments in the Soviet Union and Communist China. This approach served as the basis for Kissinger's foreign policy during the Nixon and Ford Administrations.

Kissinger considered himself a realist who favored a certain flexibility when working to advance the foreign policy interests of the United States. He called for a general policy of "détente" with the Soviet Union. "Détente," a French term with no precise English translation, worked out in a theoretical sense to mean a lessening of tensions with the Soviet Union in the hopes that stable relations would gradually lead to an improvement in the international climate. In practice, détente took the form of American loan guarantees to the Soviet government, trade and technology deals between the superpowers, and, after several years of high-level diplomacy, the opening of the Strategic Arms Limitation Talks (SALT) ultimately leading to an arms control treaty in 1972.

Ford chose to retain Kissinger as his Secretary of State, thus giving his implicit blessing to the détente policy. U.S.-Soviet relations were marked by ongoing arms control negotiations and symbolic actions such as the Apollo-Soyuz joint manned space flight. While some world leaders praised détente as a welcome respite from the hard-edged Cold War atmosphere of the period 1945-1968, others noted that, despite the supposed "lessening of tensions," the Soviets continued to engage in an adventurous foreign policy, leading to an expansion of their influence in Africa, the Middle East, and Latin America. As historian John Lewis Gaddis wrote, "Most experts would probably have agreed that it (the global balance of power) had been tilting in Moscow's favor through most of the 1970s."[31] Critics declared that Ford seemed too comfortable with the apparent retreat of American power around the world

---

[30] Cannon, *Time And Chance,* p. 400.
[31] John Lewis Gaddis, *The Cold War: A New History*, (New York: Penguin Publishing, 2005) p. 212.

during his term of office in the mid-1970s. This conviction ultimately led Ronald Reagan to challenge Ford's leadership of the GOP in 1976.

President Ford began his journey into the thickets of international diplomacy in November of 1974, when he met with Soviet leader Leonid Brezhnev at Vladivostok, concluding a nine-day trip to East Asia. Ford and Brezhnev established an immediate rapport, discussing sports such as hunting and soccer. They then moved on to the real purpose of the meeting: Consideration of an extension of the 1972 Strategic Arms Limitation Talks (SALT) agreement. Ford found Brezhnev and the Soviet team tough and experienced in the art of negotiation, but in the bargaining sessions the two sides ironed out an agreement to take another step toward limiting the spread of nuclear weapons. As Ford biographer James Cannon noted, "... all arms reductions made by his successor Presidents followed the outline of the agreement Ford negotiated at Vladivostok."[32]

Many Americans applauded Ford and his foreign policy team that Thanksgiving, but the approbation did not ring universal. In general, most conservatives, especially of the Republican variety, frowned upon the idea of détente, which grew increasingly unpopular with the public and Congress as 1974 turned to 1975. Many Republican and some conservative Democrats believed that the warming of Soviet-American relations had been accomplished by American submission to Soviet expansionist aims. As many conservatives asked: "Where does détente end and appeasement begin?"[33] Conservative firebrand Phyllis Schlafly denounced the Ford-Brezhnev agreement as the "Ambush At Vladivostok." In the Congress, Democratic Senator Henry "Scoop" Jackson of Washington led a movement to derail the treaty, which he considered inimical to American interests, in the sense that the United States would forego deployment of the Tomahawk Cruise Missile, while the Soviet Union's new Backfire Bomber was exempted from the final agreement. Governor Ronald Reagan of California, sounding evermore like a Presidential candidate, weighed in with similar concerns. The Administration, predictably, dismissed the Jackson and Reagan criticisms as political in nature, but these critiques illustrated the deep divisions in America concerning foreign policy during the mid-to-late 1970s.

Ford's greatest foreign policy misfortune came in presiding over the final collapse of the American ally in South Vietnam, and the concomitant defeat in the Vietnam War. The Vietnam crucible has been thoroughly essayed by

---

[32] Cannon, *Time And Chance*, p. 396.
[33] Gaddis, *The Cold War*, p. 210.

historians and requires no deep treatment here. Suffice to say that Ford took office and pledged to renew American military aid to South Vietnam if the Communist North Vietnamese state ever directly threatened the South Vietnamese independence, regardless of the fact that this position generated little support in domestic political circles. Significantly, Ford met with the U.S. Ambassador to South Vietnam, Graham Martin, within hours of assuming the Presidency on August 9, 1974.[34] However, a mood of war weariness suffused the country in 1974-75 and Ford understood that the nation harbored no enthusiasm for a return to armed conflict in Southeast Asia. He further realized that the Congressional Democrats would flatly refuse to appropriate money for the defense of South Vietnam.

Early in 1975, encouraged by what appeared to be a clearly diminishing American commitment to South Vietnam, the North Vietnamese initiated an open offensive and poured 300,000 troops into South Vietnamese territory. In March of 1975 Ford sent General Frederick C. Weyand, the U.S. Army Chief-of-Staff, to Saigon to assess the situation and report back to the White House. Weyand returned and reported that South Vietnam would require $722 million immediately to arm and equip the troops necessary to hold Saigon and negotiate a political end to the war.[35]

Ford addressed a joint session of Congress and requested the $722 million and a further $250 million for humanitarian assistance for Vietnamese refugees and casualties. Ford stressed that the 6,000 Americans still in Vietnam were in great danger and that the lives of tens of thousands of Vietnamese who had worked on the American side depended on the resumption of aid. Ford starkly declared, "We cannot abandon our friends."[36]

On April 14, 1975 Congressional leaders personally rejected Ford's appeal. New York's Republican Senator Jacob Javits, an old Ford colleague from their days in the House of Representatives told the President, "I will give you large sums for evacuation, but not one nickel for military aid."[37] Nine days later, on April 23, 1975 Ford conceded American defeat when he made a speech at Tulane University, saying, "... the Vietnam War is finished as far as America is concerned."[38] American military forces conducted their last mission in Vietnam on April 28-29th when Marine helicopters evacuated U.S.

---

[34] Cannon, *Time And Chance*, p. 390.
[35] Ibid. p. 397.
[36] Ibid. p. 397.
[37] Ford Timeline Documents, Found at GRFPL, Vertical File.
[38] Cannon, *Time And Chance*, p. 397.

Embassy personnel and "high risk" South Vietnamese nationals from the roof of the American Embassy, under enemy fire. Over 100,000 other pro-American Vietnamese were left to scramble for their own safety, many taking to small boats for a perilous journey across the South China Sea, in search of safe haven. Saigon, the capital city of South Vietnam, fell to North Vietnamese forces on April 30, 1975.[39]

The American position in the entirety of Indochina crashed during the spring of 1975. On April 12th Ford ordered the evacuation of the U.S. diplomatic mission in Cambodia as the Communist forces advanced on the capital city of Phnom Penh. Cambodia fell to the Communist forces five days later, on April 17, 1975. The rebels promptly installed the murderous Khmer Rouge government in power. Pol Pot, the Khmer Rouge leader, sent over a million people to "re-education camps" and forced another 2 million to flee the country. By 1978, Senator George McGovern who, as the Democratic candidate for President in 1972 had called for the immediate withdrawal of American forces from Southeast Asia now called for an American invasion of Cambodia to stop the genocide.[40] Finally, in the grim spring of 1975 the communist forces of Pathet Lao took power in Laos, ending that nation's year-old coalition government. The American effort in Southeast Asia ended in a humiliating spectacle, as all of Indochina fell under Communist rule in April of 1975. America suffered, arguably, her worst defeat since the capture and burning of Washington, the national capital, by the British in 1814.

President Ford's woes in Southeast Asia continued beyond the fall of Saigon. On May 12, 1975 Cambodian Communist forces seized an American merchant ship, the S.S. *Mayaguez* in the international waters of the Gulf of Siam, near the small island of Poulo Wai. Ford, in no mood for another perceived insult to the national honor of the United States, ordered a force of U.S. Marines to safely recover the ship's crew. In a daring rescue operation carried out two days later American forces recovered the vessel and the 39 captive crewmen. Ford ordered the rescue operation as a sign of national resolve, despite the reversal in Vietnam, and he earned great public acclaim for his action. The reassertion of American power also gave Ford a temporary, but real boost in public opinion polls. The successful conclusion of the *Mayaguez* incident came, however, at a high cost as over forty American service personnel were killed in the preparation and execution of the operation.

---

[39] Ford Timeline Documents, Found at GRFPL, Vertical File.
[40] Hayward, *The Age of Reagan,* p. 411.

The President decided to capitalize on this boost in his standing during the summer of 1975. He agreed to attend the Soviet-sponsored "Conference On Security and Co-operation In Europe" meeting in Helsinki, Finland in July. Ford's participation proved very controversial, and in fact, contributed significantly to conservative Republican discontent the following year. The conference met on July 30, 1975 and brought together the representatives of over thirty nations in the largest gathering of European heads-of-state since the Congress of Vienna in 1815. After much debate and many speeches the delegates signed agreements with the aim of reducing East-West tensions.[41] The western powers recognized Eastern European boundaries established by Soviet arms after World War II, and pledged non-interference in the internal affairs of Communist states in Eastern Europe. In exchange, the Soviets agreed to relax travel restrictions, exit visas, and communications restraints, all with the aim of improving East-West relations. The Soviets also agreed to renounce the use of force against their satellite nations. While few realized it at the time the Helsinki Accords set into motion, with the freer flow of people, ideas, and information into Eastern Europe, the forces that would ultimately undermine the Soviet Empire between 1989-1992.[42]

Still, Ford paid a price for his stand. The Helsinki Accords outraged the spokesmen of many Eastern European ethnic groups in the United States who considered the recognition of boundaries and a pledge of non-interference in "internal affairs" to be a sellout of their countrymen by the United States government. Many conservatives in the media as well as politicians in both Parties, particularly Ronald Reagan, pointed out that the Soviet pledge to allow for the free flow of information across borders meant nothing, in the concrete sense. The agreements contained no enforcement mechanism and could not be measured or quantified. Conservatives argued that the Helsinki Accords had consigned Eastern Europe to perpetual Soviet slavery in exchange for a meaningless paper agreement vainly promising liberalization behind the Iron Curtain. To add fuel to the fire, the White House, worried at offending Soviet sensibilities only weeks before the summit meeting, had refused to invite the renowned Soviet dissident writer Alexander Solzhenitsyn to meet the President. Ford, in fact, in an unguarded moment, referred to Solzhenitsyn, a Nobel Laureate, as, "... a goddamned horse's ass," although he later apologized for his ill-considered remarks.

---

[41] Gaddis, *The Cold War*, p. 188.
[42] Ibid. pp. 188-89. Also see, Cannon, *Time And Chance*, pp. 399-400.

The so-called "snubbing" of Solzhenitsyn unleashed a torrent of anti-Ford invective. Conservative critics pounced on Ford as a dullard and/or a coward, afraid to stand up to the big, bad Russians.[43] The *New York Times* passed a negative judgment on Ford's "appeasement."[44] Even those who considered the Solzhenitsyn contretemps overblown admitted that Ford seemed a little too comfortable with the apparent American retreat in the world. This seeming shrinkage of American power had begun during the Vietnam debacle in the 1960s, and had picked up speed during the 1970s. Many people, on different points of the political spectrum were beginning to ask the same question: Did détente actually mean the diminution of the United States of America?

Many conservative critics answered the question in the affirmative. They believed that Ford was, at best, a status-quo politician who did not possess a true statesmanlike vision. He could not provide the inspirational leadership necessary to lead the USA to victory in the Cold War. Such thinking mushroomed into a full-scale conservative Republican rebellion, led by an aging former Hollywood movie star-turned California Governor, by the fall of 1975.

---

43 Hayward, The Age of Reagan, p. 439. The author quotes George Will and William F. Buckley heaping scorn upon Ford.
44 Ibid. pp. 439-440.

Chapter 8

1976

As 1975 ground tediously on, Ford believed that he was growing into the Presidency, the disastrous reverse in Southeast Asia, notwithstanding. He also found, to his undoubted surprise, that he liked being the President of the United States. He thought that he was getting pretty good at his job, and he showed that the trappings of office had not gone to his head. He remained the down-to-earth fellow he had always been, especially when he shrugged off the jokes made at his expense. These involved his supposedly dim intellect and his physical clumsiness, the latter satirized constantly on the NBC weekend comedy sketch program, "Saturday Night Live," by the actor Chevy Chase. As Ford recalled in later years, "Chevy might have cost us some votes, but he was damned funny."[1]

Ford had given the country no indication of his plans beyond the end of his term in early 1977. He had purposely remained vague about any future ambitions during the first months of his Presidency as he struggled to find his stride. Now, Ford believed that he could handle the stresses of the position of Chief Executive and that he had, in fact, done a credible job in office after a rocky period immediately following the Nixon pardon. Gerald R. Ford formally announced his candidacy for the 1976 Republican Presidential nomination on July 8, 1975.[2]

If the President believed that the simple act of declaring his candidacy would clear the field of potential challengers he miscalculated, badly. Conservative disaffection for the Ford Administration was an open secret by

---

[1] Brinkley, *Gerald R. Ford,* p. 125.
[2] Gerald Ford Timeline, found at GRFPL, Vertical File.

1975.[3] The conservative wing of the GOP overlooked Ford's genuine center-right inclinations and his solidly conservative voting record while in Congress and, instead, concentrated on his alleged apostasies, calling him out for actions such as nominating Nelson Rockefeller to the Vice-Presidency. Rockefeller had feuded with the Republican conservatives for years after the bitter 1964 GOP Presidential nomination contest. Senator Barry Goldwater, the eventual Republican nominee, had long since made peace with Rockefeller, but the GOP conservatives still distrusted the New Yorker, who relished their disapproval and returned it gladly.

Conservatives considered the Rockefeller nomination a studied insult tossed at them by President Ford in one of his first official actions. Conservative Republicans also frowned on Ford's decision to retain Nixon's foreign policy team, assuming, correctly, that Kissinger would continue his détente policy with the Soviet Union. Many Americans, Republican and Democratic alike, hoped for a more assertive American foreign policy under Ford, but doubted that Kissinger would deliver one. Their suspicions deepened after the Southeast Asian debacle and reached the tipping point after what they considered to be the "sellout" of Eastern Europe, by Ford at Helsinki, in the summer of 1975. The conservative wing of the GOP decided that they had no alternative but to run a challenger against President Ford for the Republican nomination for the Presidency in 1976. Most of the conservatives agreed that the challenger should be Ronald Reagan, the former governor of California.

Conservative Republicans rallied to Reagan's standard after the former movie and television star made the transition to public life. In 1964 Reagan, a former FDR Democrat, completed a fifteen-year journey to Conservative Republicanism when he made a nationally televised speech backing Republican Presidential candidate Barry Goldwater on October 27, 1964. The following week President Lyndon Johnson crushed Goldwater in one of the most one-sided electoral contests in American history. Ronald Reagan, however, emerged as the great conservative hope, arising phoenix-like out of the ashes of the Goldwater candidacy.

Ronald Reagan, a native son of Illinois, trod an unlikely path to politics and a presidential challenge. Reagan, born in 1911 in Tampico, Illinois, grew to maturity in a number of small Prairie State towns. He graduated from Eureka College with a BA in economics in 1932. He worked a number of jobs after graduating from college and found his first promising and steady employment as a sports reporter and broadcaster for WHO Radio, in Des

---

[3] Hayward, *The Age of Reagan,* p. 253.

Moines, Iowa. WHO sent out a powerful signal and "Dutch" Reagan became a fairly familiar voice to radio-listeners in the upper Midwest. In 1937 Reagan undertook a promotional tour for WHO wherein he accompanied the Chicago Cubs to spring training on Catalina Island. While in Southern California he contacted an actress named Joy Hodges, who he had interviewed on WHO and asked her about employment possibilities in the motion picture industry. She introduced Reagan to her agent, who arranged a screen test at Warner Brothers' studio. The studio bosses liked what they saw and offered the erstwhile sportscaster a seven-year contract, paying him $200.00 per week, a handsome salary for a country still fighting the Great Depression.[4]

After relocating to Hollywood, Reagan starred in numerous films, mostly forgettable. He did, however, earn a reputation as a solid and capable professional actor. He showed up on time, knew his lines, accepted direction graciously, and his winning personality made him one of the more popular individuals in the business. Reagan earned critical acclaim for his work in the 1942 drama *King's Row* and he served as the President of the Screen Actors Guild during the 1940s and early 50s. He made the transition from movies to television easily, serving as a TV actor and corporate spokesman for General Electric.[5]

Reagan passed seamlessly from show business to public life in the early 1960s. By this time television had become increasingly important in American politics, and mastering the medium in the sense of confidently projecting one's ideas and personality had become essential. Reagan proved to be a master of communication, arguably the greatest Presidential orator of the 20th Century. President Ford, himself, admired Reagan's skills as a communicator of ideas. Journalist Thomas De Frank remembered Ford discussing Reagan in 1976 and admitting, "He had a hell of a flair."[6]

It would have been a mistake, however, to dismiss Reagan as simply an actor, although many, including Presidents Ford and Carter, made that mistake. By 1976 Reagan had spent over ten years in national politics. He read voraciously and he wrote widely on a multitude of topics. Reagan also served two successful terms as the governor of California. The "Golden State" the most populous state in the union, boasted an economy that would have rated as the seventh largest in the world, if considered apart from the other 49 states.

---

[4] Jules Tygiel, *Ronald Reagan And The Triumph of American Conservatism*, (New York: Pearson/Longman, 2006) pp. 28-34

[5] Ibid. pp. 87-97.

[6] DeFrank, *Write It When I'm Gone*, p. 122.

Serving as the governor of California conferred upon an individual the true executive experience necessary for the Presidency.[7]

Reagan had mulled over a Presidential bid in 1976, when he assumed Nixon would be leaving office. Ford's accession to the Presidency upset the calculations, however, and Reagan hesitated to challenge an incumbent President from his own Party. Reagan publicly expressed disagreement with the seeming drift of the Ford foreign policy in 1974-75, and the last straw was Ford's refusal to meet with the famed Russian dissident writer Alexander Solzhenitsyn. In his syndicated newspaper column Reagan severely chastised Ford for practicing appeasement of the Soviets concerning this matter. He ridiculed the White House spokespeople for the evasive nature of their reasons why Ford could not meet with Solzhenitsyn, a Nobel Prize winning author, who illustrated, in stark terms, the horrors of Communism. Reagan further informed his readers that he would have considered it an honor to meet with a survivor of the Soviet prison camps.

Reagan made his decision to run for the Republican nomination for the Presidency and informed Ford of this fact in a private telephone call. He publicly announced his candidacy for the Republican nomination for the Presidency of the United States of America on November 20, 1975.[8] Ford later claimed that he was stunned when Reagan informed him of his decision to run for President. Jerry Ford cannot be taken at his word in this instance. Reagan had harbored unconcealed Presidential ambitions for years and all of his speeches in 1974-75 sounded like those of a Presidential candidate. At any rate the coming contest promised to be a very bitter mortal combat. Reagan thought of Ford as a political innocent, in over his head as the President. Ford, according to his journalist friend Thomas DeFrank, "… neither liked nor respected the former Hollywood actor. He considered Reagan a superficial, disengaged, intellectually lazy showman who didn't do his homework and clung to a naïve, unrealistic and essentially dangerous worldview."[9] Ford made up his mind that he would campaign as hard as necessary to win the nomination, even though he suspected that the coming battle would deeply scar his beloved Republican Party.

As the campaign unfolded, Ford worked the levers of incumbency and power, while Reagan fed off of the energy of his conservative faithful. On February 26, 1976 Ford upset the slightly favored challenger by a scant 1,250

---

[7] Schwiekart and Allen, A Patriot's History of the United States, pp. 744-745.
[8] Gerald Ford Timeline Documents, found at GRFPL, Vertical File.
[9] DeFrank, Write It When I'm Gone, p. 122.

votes in the New Hampshire primary, the nation's first primary election. The President took 17 out of 21 possible delegates. Ford went on to easy wins in Massachusetts, Vermont, Florida and Illinois and seemed ready to lock up the nomination. Ford had his challenger on the ropes and many Republicans, including longtime conservative stalwart Barry Goldwater, publicly urged Reagan to concede the race.

Reagan fired back at Ford in North Carolina and found a receptive audience. He dropped his "nice guy" strategy and concentrated on highly charged issues like détente and the proposed Panama Canal treaties, which Reagan characterized as a "giveaway" of American territory. On March 23rd Reagan won the Tar Heel State by a 54-46% vote and took a majority of the delegates. He reeled off a string of victories, sweeping the Texas delegates, and rolling up solid majorities in Georgia, Alabama, and Indiana. In a surprise win, Missouri Republicans ignored the express wishes of state Party leaders like Governor Christopher S. Bond and U.S. Senate nominee John Danforth and awarded Reagan 19 out of the state's 30 delegates. The momentum had now definitely shifted to the challenger and he posed the most credible, even serious threat to an incumbent Republican President since Theodore Roosevelt challenged William Howard Taft in 1912.[10]

The primary campaign seesawed back and forth with neither candidate able to establish a lasting lead. At the beginning of June the two contenders were virtually deadlocked. Reagan won the California primary, which was expected in his home state. The following week Ford took 60% of the vote in Ohio, winning 91 out of 97 delegates. The momentum had now shifted back to the incumbent President. As the campaign moved toward the nominating convention Ford held his slight lead. Seeking to shore up his faltering campaign, Reagan named Richard Schweiker, a moderately liberal U.S. Senator from Pennsylvania as his Vice-Presidential running mate. Reagan sought to sway certain wavering delegates, but his gambit fell flat. Ford held his lead and continued his progress toward a first ballot nomination as the convention neared.

The Republicans met in convention at Kansas City, Missouri but the event turned out to be somewhat anti-climactic. Ford managed to hold onto his delegates and defeated Reagan on the first ballot by a roll call vote of 1187-1070, one of the closest convention votes in decades. Reagan supporters staged a passionate hour-long demonstration for their champion on nomination night, to no avail. Ford gave his acceptance speech and, in response to pleas

---

[10] Edwards, *The Conservative Revolution*, p. 203.

from some delegates, he graciously invited Reagan to the rostrum to address the convention. Reagan delivered a rhetorical masterpiece, without notes or teleprompter, causing the entire convention to break into wild applause. Ford, sadly, found himself upstaged at his own nominating convention.[11]

Reagan sent word to the Ford camp that he had no interest in the Vice-Presidency, which came as a great relief to the President and his team. After the bitterness of the campaign, which lingered for a number of years, Ford did not want Reagan on the ticket and the two men clearly could not have worked together in a productive and harmonious fashion.[12] Ford turned to Bob Dole, the senior U.S. Senator from Kansas, as his Vice-Presidential running mate. Ford knew and trusted Dole and believed that he could deliver the agricultural mid-western states that were crucial to a Republican victory. Dole, a moderate-conservative like Ford, himself, carried a reputation as a strong campaigner with a quick wit, although this showed itself rarely during the campaign.

How do historians evaluate the Ford-Reagan nomination battle? First of all, the fact that Reagan challenged Ford and ran well indicated a distinct weakness in Ford's appeal. Ford and many of his advisers (as well as historians like Douglas Brinkley) dismissed the Reagan challenge as merely an exercise in egotism by the Californian. However, the strength of Reagan's challenge illustrated the yearning of a substantial faction in the GOP for a new and bolder approach to public life rather than the politics-as-usual approach exemplified by President Ford and his newly minted running mate, Senator Bob Dole. In fact, the 1976 campaign provided a preview of the massive shift, if not realignment developing in American politics. Reagan appealed to those outside of the slim Republican economic conservative base. The conservative candidate actually introduced Republican politics to those who would later be labeled "social conservatives," people who generally voted Democratic. Ford, playing the game safely, resorted to a tired GOP strategy of attempting to eke out a victory by prying a few moderate liberals loose from the Democrats and adding them to the habitual Republican base. As journalist William Rusher said, "... Ford simply had no comprehension of the seismic forces at work in American politics."[13]

Ford bitterly resented Reagan's challenge and harbored a certain level of ill will for a number of years thereafter. Ford insisted in later years that he and

---

[11] Ibid. pp. 204-205.
[12] Cannon, *Time And Chance*, p. 49.
[13] Rusher, *The Rise of The Right*, p. 264.

Reagan had made peace but Ford always believed that Reagan had cost him the presidency in 1976. As Thomas DeFrank recalled, "In his public comments over the years he (Ford) usually listed Reagan's pro forma campaigning as one of several factors in his defeat ..."[14] Ford claimed that he would have won in Missouri, Mississippi, and Wisconsin if Reagan had been willing to campaign for the GOP ticket in those states. Victory in those states would have pushed Ford over the 270 electoral vote threshold necessary to win the Presidency. Many historians and political scientists contest the idea that Reagan sat out the 1976 general election campaign.[15] Ford, however, remained unshakeable in his conviction that Reagan's tepid support in the fall of 1976 cost the GOP the election.

The Democrats nominated Jimmy Carter, a former Georgia governor and Democratic National Committee chairman as their 1976 Presidential candidate. Carter's victory in the Democratic nomination derby surprised many people; a popular tagline during the 1976 primary season was: "Jimmy Who?" He projected an air of small-town American decency and probity, but behind the regular guy image laid a cunning, intensely ambitious, and calculating politician. Carter had compiled a sgenerally credible record as Georgia governor, had used his position as DNC Chairman to develop contacts with every Democratic officeholder and interest group in the country, and had made fortuitous acquaintances overseas. While he remained a question mark to the majority of the American people, Carter had actually become a fairly well known figure in key Democratic circles by that time. He chose to run for the Presidency, thinking the time was right for a self-professed "ordinary guy" from Georgia, an outsider who would bring small town virtues to Babylon-On-The-Potomac.

Carter, however, worried many people. He seemed to stand for nothing concrete and spoke largely in platitudes. His folksy style impressed some observers as practiced and inauthentic. Many journalists detected a distinct coldness of character behind the ever-present Carter smile. Arthur Schlesinger, Jr., the renowned historian and Democratic partisan, confided to his diary on February 16, 1976, "... I must confess he (Carter) continues to turn me off, his steely eyes, fixed grin, righteousness, and ambiguity on the issues."[16] Bill Moyers, the former Lyndon Johnson aide and PBS pundit, opined that Carter

---

[14] DeFrank, Write It When I'm Gone, p. 123.

[15] Tygiel, Ronald Reagan, p. 133.

[16] Arthur M. Schlesinger, Jr. Journals 1952-2000, (New York: Penguin Publishing, 2007) p. 407.

was "… a Calvinist … the sort who would burn people at the stake."[17] Yet, Carter and the Democrats scented victory in 1976 and the early pre-campaign polls showed them leading the Ford-Dole ticket by 34 percentage points.[18]

Ford and his campaign team approached the campaign and the election with a quiet confidence, but they also realized that they would have to work hard to make up the deficit. The Ford team understood their boss and his weaknesses. Stu Spencer, the President's campaign manager, told him to his face, "Mr. President, as a campaigner, you're no (blasted) good."[19] Gradually, the campaign team decided to play up the theme of Ford as a responsible and effective President, while attempting to sow public doubts about Carter and his readiness to assume the Presidency. Ford used this modified "Rose Garden" strategy well and nearly succeeded in pulling of a huge upset in November of 1976.

Ford's first foray away from the White House and onto the campaign trail proved a disappointment. On September 15, 1976 Ford officially launched his campaign by making an appearance at his alma mater, the University of Michigan at Ann Arbor. The campaign managers obviously chose to put their man in a friendly setting, hoping to maximize favorable publicity. According to one eyewitness, the celebrated journalist Robert Novak, the effort flatly failed. "… It was an uncomfortable meeting for the '76 Wolverines and the old grad, the class of '35, former football captain. Bo Shembechler, Michigan's uptight football coach, was displeased with the distraction, and the players seemed uninterested in dining with the President of the United States. Although he was a big man, the players dwarfed him. Ford, seeming ill at ease, made no attempt to break the ice with the players."[20] Ford's speech the following day amounted to a turgid recitation of the names of federal programs thrown together and presented as a "new vision for America."

In 1988, the sitting Vice-President and newly nominated Republican candidate for the Presidency of the United States George H.W. Bush spoke dismissively about "the vision thing". Bush took a cue from his mentor, the Thirty-Eighth President of the United States, Gerald R. Ford, when it came to the "vision thing." Ford, who had made a career out of being non-ideological and practical by nature, showed that his lack of philosophical certitude confirmed the fact that he had no overarching agenda, no clear inspiration for

---

[17] Ibid. p. 209.
[18] Novak, *The Prince of Darkness*, p. 281.
[19] Cannon, *Time And Chance*, p. 407.
[20] Novak, *The Prince of Darkness*, p. 291.

his country, and had really no "vision" for the future and for America. After the muddle in Ann Arbor the campaign team decided to keep Ford's appearances highly scripted and structured. Ford's lack of any real agenda remained an open secret, but one that his side attempted to conceal.

The campaign ground forward and, as Republican strategists hoped, the electorate began to question the Democratic nominee and his readiness to assume the Presidency. Slowly, but surely, the Ford-Dole ticket began to creep up in the polls. Governor Carter nearly ruined his image as a strong family man in an ill-advised interview with *Playboy* Magazine, using salty language unsuited to his supposed God-fearing persona. Bad economic news in September somewhat dampened GOP spirits, but the President's campaign squad placed their hope on Ford's performance in three prime time made-for-television debates between the candidates.

The series of three televised debates between the candidates returned in 1976 after a sixteen-year hiatus. The famed Kennedy-Nixon debates of 1960 had transfixed the country, and had shown the growing power of television to influence, for better or worse, public perceptions of candidates. The studies of the 1960 campaign showed that a slim majority of those who listened to the debates on radio thought that Nixon had outpointed his challenger. A clear majority, however, of those who had watched the contests on television thought that Kennedy, who appeared cool and calm during these affairs, had gotten the better of the exchanges. In 1976, the Ford camp challenged Carter to a series of debates, hoping to point out the Georgian's relative lack of experience, particularly on foreign and defense policy matters. No responsible member of the Ford campaign thought to warn the GOP side of the dangers of elevating the challenger by debating face-to-face, nor did they heed the historical precedent of 1960, whereby a challenger could prove his mettle by simply avoiding an unfortunate *faux pas*.

The candidates first squared off in Philadelphia on September 23, 1976 in a debate on domestic and economic issues. This first Presidential debate in sixteen years turned out well for Ford, as most viewers called it a "win" for the GOP candidate. Jimmy Carter seemed nervous and unsure of himself, while Ford rose above his usual plodding speaking style to answer questions in a forthright and substantive manner.[21] The public reaction to this debate gave Ford and the GOP ticket a boost in the polls, which showed an increasingly close race. Ford and his campaign staff, gaining confidence, now looked

---

[21] Hayward, *The Age of Reagan*, p. 501.

forward to the second debate, on foreign policy and defense issues, set for October 6th, in San Francisco.

Presidential debates provide good political theater but rarely turn an election. The candidates perform guardedly, seldom giving the opponent any ammunition and almost never blundering badly. The second debate of the 1976 Presidential derby, however, gave Jimmy Carter and the Democrats a huge boost and, some historians would argue, the key to election victory. Panelist and questioner Max Frankel of the *New York Times* asked Ford whether détente, as illustrated by SALT and the Helsinki Accords, benefited the Soviet Union and constrained the USA. Frankel's question touched on the familiar objection that the Helsinki agreements had ceded Eastern Europe to the Soviet Union. Ford responded to the question with the astounding statement, "There is no Soviet domination of Eastern Europe and there never will be under a Ford Administration." The breathtaking foolishness of that statement undid all of the campaign staffers efforts to make Ford appear Presidential and commanding, and, in fact, reawakened all of the old doubts about the President's own intelligence.[22] On live television the President of the United States insisted that the Soviet Union did not dominate Eastern Europe. Worse yet, when Frankel gave the President a line of retreat from this declaration, Ford dug himself in deeper, maintaining that Yugoslavians, Romanians, and Poles did not consider themselves dominated by the Soviets. This single statement lost the Eastern European ethnic vote in the upcoming election.[23]

The misstatement provided comic fodder for the rest of the election campaign. Ford's revised explanation of the remark to mean that the Unites States did not accept the legitimacy of the Soviet armed dominance of Eastern Europe vanished in the gales of laughter concerning the ridiculous nature of the assertion. The public could only conclude that Ford was dense, or that he deliberately ignored reality. *National Review*, editor William F. Buckley referred to Ford's gaffe as, "The ultimate Polish joke."[24]

There can be no doubt that the "Eastern Europe" remark badly hurt the Ford re-election campaign. The President's halting and slow speaking style handicapped his electioneering and, when paired with a gross misstatement of fact, it raised questions about the candidate's grasp of reality. The continuing fallout about the Eastern Europe statement dominated the campaign news as

---

[22] Brinkley, *Gerald R. Ford*, pp. 142-143.
[23] Novak, *The Prince of Darkness*, pp. 293-294.
[24] William F. Buckley Jr., quoted in Brinkley, *Gerald R. Ford*, p. 143.

October wore on. The third candidate debate passed uneventfully at Williamsburg, Virginia on October 22nd. Heading into the final weekend of the campaign the polls showed a statistical dead heat. The final Harris Poll showed Carter leading by one point, while a Gallup Poll put Ford ahead by the same margin.[25] Despite the Eastern Europe gaffe and the President's colorless speaking style, the campaign had made up a thirty-four point deficit in the polls.

On Saturday, October 30th, Ford made a campaign speech in Houston and hustled to another event in Philadelphia. He then videotaped a campaign commercial to the American people, which ran on Monday, November 1, 1976, the eve of the election. Ford returned to Grand Rapids to attend his final rally on that same Monday, November 1st. He cast his vote on the morning of November 2nd, attended the unveiling of a "Gerald Ford Mural" at the Kent County (Michigan) airport and flew back to Washington.

Ford joined family, staff, and close friends including Joe Garigiola, the ex-major league baseball star and popular NBC sportscaster, in the White House family quarters on election night to watch the returns. The watch party saw Carter take an early lead and doggedly hold this edge for the rest of the evening. Ford retired to bed at 3:15 AM (Eastern Standard Time) with the outcome still undecided, but the odds against a Republican victory. The next morning, Ford's head staffer, Dick Cheney, met the boss in the Oval Office and gave him the grim news, "Mr. President, we lost."[26]

Ford had given the campaign his all, but the Republican ticket fell just short. Carter took 40.8 million votes to Ford's 39.1 million. The President won in the West and ran very strongly in the Midwest, as well. President-Elect Carter swept the South, with the exception of Virginia, and rolled up large margins in the urban East, to forge his victory. The Electoral College vote broke down at 297-240 for Carter, with one vote going to Ronald Reagan. It turned out to be the closest electoral vote since 1916.

Ford, showing the sense of class the nation had now grown to expect as a matter of course, wrote a concession statement and immediately placed a call to Jimmy Carter. Ford, hoarse from the final rigors of the campaign trail, greeted the victor, passed his congratulations, and then directed Dick Cheney to write a formal concession statement. Due to the hoarseness in his voice, the President had his wife, Betty, read the statement for the television cameras.

---

[25] Brinkley, *Gerald R. Ford*, p. 144.
[26] Cannon, *Time And Chance*, p. 408.

Ford found his electoral defeat a deflating experience and he was terribly disappointed by the 1976 loss. The 1976 defeat would rank as his only setback; he had never before been rejected by the electorate, and had won each previous race handily. By his own estimate, the loss threw him into a "funk" that lasted for a full month after the election. He replayed the campaign in his own mind, poring over the "what-ifs," saving particular scorn for Ronald Reagan, believing that the Ford-Dole team would have won if Reagan had put aside his own disappointment and campaigned for the Party and the national ticket.[27]

Ford spent the remainder of 1976 attending to the national business and preparing for life after the Presidency. On December 14th Ford sent a letter to the Archivist of the United States and a copy to the President of the University of Michigan, offering to donate his personal and public papers to a proposed library to be built on the University of Michigan campus. Ford delivered his final formal State address on January 12, 1977. Despite some disquieting economic statistics he reported that the general state of the American union was good. Ford claimed the credit, as any politician would, for the supposed improvement in the national condition saying, "… today we have a more perfect union then when my stewardship began."[28] While some criticized the apparently self-serving nature of this statement, most of the national political class gave Ford belated credit for his efforts. On January 20, 1977 Ford formally relinquished the Presidency, handing the institution over to his erstwhile opponent, Jimmy Carter. In his inaugural address Carter magnanimously stated, "For myself and for our nation, I want to thank my predecessor for all he has done to heal our land."[29]

---

[27] Ford, *A Time To Heal,* pp. 424, 437.
[28] Gerald R. Ford Timeline Documents, found at GRFPL, Vertical File.
[29] Ibid.

Chapter 9

RETIREMENT

Literally dozens of well-wishers greeted the Fords as they prepared to depart Washington after the inauguration of President Carter. After accepting the farewells of many acquaintances and wishing the best to all of the friends they had made in twenty-eight years of government service, Jerry and Betty Ford, now private citizens, boarded Marine One, the private helicopter for the short hop to Andrews Air Force Base. They would then jet to Houston for a speaking appearance, and on to their retirement home at Rancho Mirage, California, a relatively new desert resort community near Palm Springs. The former First Couple apparently never seriously considered returning "home" to Grand Rapids after leaving Washington, despite the fact that they had represented the district in Congress for over a quarter-century, and Ford proudly referred to himself as a "Michigander."

Once the Marine copter launched, Ford asked the pilot to circle the Capitol, instead of the White House. "That's my real home," he remarked wistfully.[1] The Fords eventually made their way to the retirement residence in California. They split time between Rancho Mirage and a vacation condominium in Vail, Colorado. This routine gave the ex-President the opportunity to indulge two of his favorite passions: skiing in the winter, and golf whenever the weather permitted. The former world-class athlete still thrilled at the competition of sport, and he now had plenty of time for action.

Gradually, Ford worked out a regimen as an ex-President. In March of 1977 he and Betty signed contracts to publish their memoirs, which each completed in 1979. Ford participated in various charitable causes, particularly

---

[1] Brinkley, *Gerald R. Ford*, p.146.

celebrity golf tournaments with friends like Arnold Palmer and Bob Hope. He also remained involved in national and international causes, although he preferred to keep a low profile and work behind the scenes in such affairs. Ford did not seek the spotlight and he very rarely criticized sitting Presidents. He remained a significant influence in moderate Republican circles during his retirement, and stressed his centrist leanings, which belies the insistence of certain historians, notably Douglas Brinkley, that Ford was strongly conservative.

In addition to the compensation derived from the contracts to write memoirs, ex-President Ford moved quickly to develop real financial security, a luxury he had never known as a congressman, even though he had held a leadership position. As an ex-President, Ford drew a $100,000 yearly pension. He supplemented this income with fees from speaking engagements, particularly in the first few years after his term of office. He also lent his name to corporations eager to have a prominent public figure on their masthead and payroll. In short order, Ford took positions on the Boards of Directorships of numerous companies, including American Express, Shearson/AMEX, Santa Fe International, Texas Commerce Bank and 20th Century Fox Film Corporation.[2] Positions on these corporate boards paid Ford well over a million dollars a year, which, when added to his speaking fees, pension, book contract, and royalties made the ex-President and First Lady a very wealthy retired couple.

Some observers, including journalists and political scientists, noted the example of ex-President Harry S. Truman spending retirement in near-poverty in Missouri, and accused Ford of "selling out" to corporate America, and of profiting in a somewhat unseemly fashion for the mere fortuity of having been the President of the United States. Ford cavalierly dismissed such criticism, saying, "I'm a private citizen now. It's nobodies business."[3] While this may have been true in the strictest sense, some believed that it tarnished Ford's formerly sterling reputation for integrity.

Personal difficulties also sullied what Jerry and Betty Ford hoped would be a carefree retirement. Betty Ford had struggled with painkiller and alcohol addiction since her bout with breast cancer. She did not make the transition from public figure to private citizen easily, later admitting that she plunged into a deep depression after leaving Washington in early 1977. This seems to have been a case of empty nest syndrome, with the family members now going

---

[2] Gerald R. Ford Timeline Documents, found at GRFPL, Vertical File.
[3] Brinkley, *Gerald R. Ford*, p. 152.

their separate ways, and Betty admitted in later years that she felt a disturbing sense of alienation and uprootedness, upon leaving Washington, saying that the District of Columbia had been the only home that the family had ever really known. She sought solace in alcohol and soon developed an addiction to prescription painkillers.

After a family intervention on April 11, 1978 Mrs. Ford entered the Long Beach Naval Hospital for chemical dependency treatment. The ex-President spent as much time at his wife's bedside as possible, and, in order to show his sense of loyalty, he gave up his martinis and his Scotch whiskey. Later he worked with Betty and their longtime friend, Ambassador Leonard Firestone, to establish a modern detoxification and rehabilitation center. The family dedicated the Betty Ford Clinic for the treatment of chemical dependency at the Eisenhower Medical Center in Palm Springs, a few miles from their retirement home at Rancho Mirage, on October 3, 1982.[4]

Ford viewed the political scene of the mid-to-late 1970s with growing dismay. He had handed the Presidency over to Jimmy Carter with grace and dignity and had literally prayed for Carter's success. Like the majority of Americans, though, Ford reacted negatively to the many difficulties that plagued the nation during the Carter Administration. Long lines at the gasoline pumps, double-digit inflation, the recession of 1979-80, Soviet-Cuban adventurism in Africa and Central America, the Russian invasion of Afghanistan, and the seemingly endless Iran hostage crisis convinced Ford that Jimmy Carter was out of his depth as the President of the United States. At this point, Ford began to actively consider a second Presidential nomination and a possible rematch with Carter in 1980.

Ford's motives in considering a 1980 Presidential race sprang from a mixture of pragmatism, ideology, and ordinary human vanity. He believed that Carter had "... fumbled the ball," in broad terms, translated to mean that the Georgian had simply failed to meet the challenges of the Presidency. Ideologically speaking, Ford figured that the nation would benefit from his center-right approach, rather than the center-left approach that he believed defined the Carter style. Ford also worried that the unabashed conservatism of his old Republican rival Ronald Reagan could sink the GOP, if left unchecked in the coming electoral cycle. On a personal level, Ford longed to remove the asterisk next to his name in the history books, by winning the Presidency in his own right. He wanted to even the score with Carter and, as Thomas DeFrank

---

[4] Gerald R. Ford Timeline Documents, found at GRPFL, Vertical File.

has written, "... he also relished the payback prospect of denying the Oval Office to Reagan, whom he considered a lazy and unfit pretender."[5]

Ford's old loyalists were split on the idea. Henry Kissinger and former Air Force Secretary Thomas Reed urged him to run, even forming a "Draft Ford" committee. Governors Jim Rhodes of Ohio and Bob Clement of Texas, states indispensable to a GOP presidential candidate, urged him to throw his hat in the ring. Still, Ford partisans like Dick Cheney, Stuart Spencer, and Bob Teeter advised otherwise, knowing that every variable would have to break Ford's way and that the team would have a bitter battle with Ronald Reagan, who could not have been expected to step aside for the ex-President, although Ford thought, incredibly, that Reagan should have simply withdrawn his candidacy, given up his own Presidential aspirations, and let Ford take another shot at Carter! As Thomas DeFrank recounted, "He (Ford) emphatically told me, moreover, that Reagan should have graciously stepped aside in 1980 so he could run against Jimmy Carter again and was monumentally irked when he didn't."[6]

In early March of 1980, with the primary season well underway and important filing deadlines looming, Ford met with his unofficial committee at Rancho Mirage. The political numbers crunchers delivered the bad news that they would fall at least 150 delegates short of catching Reagan. His old stalwarts stated that they would support him if he ran, but warned him of the difficulties ahead, including the possibility that a bitter Republican split could ensure a Democratic victory and Carter's re-election in November. Ford, realizing that his time had come and gone, decided to give up the ghost.

On Saturday, March 15, 1980 Gerald Ford officially took himself out of consideration for the Republican nomination for the Presidency. He informed the reporters, "America needs a new President. I have determined that I can best help that cause, by not being a candidate for President, which might further divide my Party ..."[7] He pledged to support the GOP nominee with all of his energy. In later years Ford called this the hardest decision of his life.[8]

The attraction of high office continued to lure Ford even after he ruled out another Presidential run. In June of 1980 representatives of the presumptive GOP nominee, Ronald Reagan, met with representatives of the Ford camp and considered the possibility of having ex-President Ford run as the Vice-

---

[5] DeFrank, Write It When I'm Gone, p. 89.
[6] Ibid. p. 123.
[7] Gerald R. Ford Timeline Documents, found at GRFPL, Vertical File.
[8] Ibid.

Presidential candidate on the Republican ticket. At the Republican convention at Detroit in July of 1980 Reagan personally approached Ford and asked him to consider the Vice-Presidency. Agents from each camp attempted to work out the details of a Reagan-Ford ticket, but Ford demanded an arrangement amounting to a "co-presidency" with himself having great power over the federal budget and economic policymaking. Ford's demands for unprecedented power broke the momentum of the deal and the negotiations ended on an officially amicable note, although the parties involved showed a noticeable coolness toward each other after the deal broke down. Despite the fact that Ford did not join the ticket several major newspapers reported otherwise, and CBS news anchor Walter Cronkite announced to the nation, "… it will be Ford," on his evening broadcast from the Detroit convention. The Vice-Presidential slot on the Republican ticket was eventually filled by Ford's own preferred candidate, George H.W. Bush.[9]

Ford, the loyal Party man, stumped for Reagan during the 1980 campaign, in a somewhat self-conscious fashion since he blamed his 1976 loss on Reagan's supposed inactivity on the campaign trail. Ford decided to lead by example and actively supported his onetime rival. On Sunday, November 2nd, Ford appeared on the NBC television program "Meet The Press" and criticized Carter for his handling of the Iran Hostage Crisis. He also offered a final appeal for candidate Reagan, saying, "Believe me, Ronnie and I had our differences. But he will be better than Carter."[10] During the two-term Reagan Administration, Ford served the President as a representative at the funeral of assassinated Egyptian President Anwar Sadat, and as an emissary in a number of unofficial capacities.

Throughout the early years of his retirement Ford worked on raising funds for the Gerald Ford Presidential Library, on the University of Michigan campus, which opened on April 27, 1981 and the Gerald Ford Presidential Museum, located at Grand Rapids, which opened on September 18, 1981. Ford was the first President since Herbert Hoover to dedicate separate facilities as a museum and a repository for official government documents.[11] Ford also put aside his lingering animosity toward his old opponent Jimmy Carter during these years and the two ex-Presidents stuck up an acquaintance that eventually warmed into friendship. Carter took part in conferences and seminars at the

---

[9] Hayward, *The Age of Reagan*, pp. 665-671.
[10] Brinkley, *Gerald R. Ford*, p. 151.
[11] Ibid. p. 152.

Ford library, while Ford reciprocated by presiding over similar events at the Carter Center in Atlanta.

During the late 1980s and on into the 1990s Ford scaled back some of his corporate work and his speaking schedule. He had earned a comfortable living and now ranked as a millionaire, many times over, so financial security no longer rated as a pressing need. Ford found the demands of travel and the routine of living out of hotel rooms more trying than in the past. He began to devote more time to activities consistent with his new, but largely undefined role as an "elder statesman." In 1987, Ford published a book entitled, *Humor and the Presidency* that he basically drew from a September 1986 conference at the Ford Presidential Museum. In 1989 he participated in a symposium at Hofstra University, which studied his Presidency and accomplishments. Years after the fact Ford found the respect that had eluded him while in office.

In the 1990s Ford wrote occasional Op-Ed pieces for the major newspapers and remained a voice in Republican moderate circles. He spoke on behalf of his former running mate Bob Dole in 1996, at the Republican Convention in San Diego, when Dole was chosen as the GOP Presidential nominee. Dole asked Ford to campaign actively on his behalf, but age and declining stamina kept Ford at home, unable to take a full role on the campaign trail for his old friend and confidant.

Ford had one final role to play on the national stage in December of 1998. As the U.S. Congress debated impeachment charges against President Clinton for perjury and other offenses in the Monica Lewinsky affair, Ford urged Congress to "rebuke" the President for his conduct in the scandal. Ford, ever the straight arrow moralist, found President Clinton's actions in the wake of his sexual affair with the twenty-year old White House intern deplorable, but not sufficiently criminal to warrant an impeachment proceeding. In a December 21, 1998 *New York Times* piece, written two days after the House voted impeachment charges against the President, Ford and his co-author, Jimmy Carter, argued for a bi-partisan resolution of censure directed against Clinton, as an alternative to the unsightly spectacle of an impeachment trial. The ex-Presidents proposed that President Clinton should appear in the Senate Chambers and accept a scolding from the legislators. The President would accept full responsibility for his actions and for attempting to delay and to impede the investigations pertaining to them. As Ford wrote, there could be, "... no spinning, no semantics, no evasiveness, or blaming others for his plight."[12] Ford and Carter's effort availed nothing as the House of

---

[12] DeFrank, Write It When I'm Gone, p. 142.

Representatives impeached President Clinton anyway; he handily won acquittal in a Senate vote in February of 1999. Clinton walked away with no official reprimand, and White House aides reported that he immediately boasted gleefully about "beating the rap."[13]

Interestingly enough, Ford's sudden intercession on Clinton's behalf began with a request from Clinton for assistance in the wake of the looming impeachment. Ford and the President had grown quite friendly by 1998, actually being on a first name basis. Clinton had called Ford in the fall of 1998 and requested his help in trying to stave off the impeachment proceeding. Ford offered to assist the President, but stated that, as a precondition, Clinton would admit to having committed perjury during the investigation. Clinton's angry refusal of the precondition ended any possibility of further collaboration between Ford and the sitting President.[14]

While the two men no longer worked together to fend off Clinton's impeachment they remained personally cordial and friendly. On August 11, 1999 President Clinton awarded Ford a Presidential Medal of Freedom, the nation's highest civilian honor, and on October 27, 1999 the Congress paid tribute to Ford by presenting him the Congressional Gold Medal, the highest legislative branch award.[15] Ford capped off this bevy of official distinctions by winning the "Profile In Courage Award," conferred by the John F. Kennedy Foundation, in 2001. Caroline Kennedy, daughter of the slain thirty-fifth President, and the head of the foundation, personally recommended Ford for the honor, and specifically cited his decision to pardon Richard Nixon in 1974 as the act of courage necessary for award consideration. Ford deemed this honor as the ultimate vindication, but it turned out to be more than recognition that he had done the right thing a quarter century earlier. It actually showed that Ford had emerged as a nationally beloved figure.

As time wore on, however, Ford's remarkable vigor visibly waned and his public appearances decreased markedly. In April of 1994 Ford joined President Clinton along with former Presidents Bush, Reagan, and Carter at the funeral of Richard Nixon. It would be the last time these men would meet together publicly. When Ronald Reagan died in June of 2004, Ford, in increasingly frail health, made the journey to Washington for the State Funeral, but could not deliver a eulogy at the service. The end, though long in coming, was drawing nearer. On November 14, 2006 Ford became the nation's

---

[13] Ibid. pp. 145-147.
[14] Ibid. p. 147.
[15] Gerald F. Ford Timeline Documents, found at GRFPL, Vertical File.

longest-lived President, surpassing his old rival/friend Ronald Reagan. Ford's health, though, was beginning to fail. He spent time in the hospital twice in 2006 for heart problems. Age had begun to crack Ford's iron constitution.

In early December of 2006 Vice-President Dick Cheney telephoned Ford to deliver the news that Congress had approved legislation naming CVN-78, the Navy's next nuclear aircraft carrier, the USS *Gerald R. Ford*. Cheney remarked that Ford was very pleased, but that he couldn't speak more than a few words at a time, and that the President's son, Steve Ford, filled in the gaps of conversation on a telephone extension. The word seeped out that Ford was reaching the end-of-the-line. By December his vital organs began to shut down, and congestive heart failure weakened his immune system, making it impossible to fight off any more infections.

Gerald R. Ford, born Leslie Lynch King, in Omaha, Nebraska died on December 26, 2006 at 6:45 PM, Pacific Standard Time. Betty and their three sons were at his bedside; daughter Susan had returned to Albuquerque, New Mexico to spend the Yuletide with her family. The Ford sons insisted that their father's last act of will consisted of not dying on Christmas Day. The family held a funeral service at St. Margaret's Church at Palm Desert, California.

During the national period of mourning the government arranged to transport President Ford's body to Washington to lie in state at the U.S. Capitol building, and for services at the National Cathedral. The December 30th funeral procession made stops at the Ford family home in Alexandria, Virginia and at the World War II Veterans Memorial before proceeding to the Capitol. Ford had specifically requested that his funeral service be a low-key and understated affair, befitting his persona. The family acceded to his wishes and celebrated a non-state funeral on January 2, 2007. President George W. Bush delivered the primary eulogy and was seconded by his father, former President George H.W. Bush, former Secretary of State Henry Kissinger and television journalist Tom Brokaw. Finally, on January 3, 2007 the family held a funeral service at Grace Episcopal Church in Grand Rapids, Michigan. Former President Jimmy Carter, old Ford loyalist and former Defense Secretary Donald Rumsfeld, and historian Richard Norton Smith articulated eulogies at the memorial. Following the service President Ford's body was laid to rest on the grounds of the Ford Presidential Museum in Grand Rapids.[16]

How will history remember Gerald R. Ford and his Presidency? The preliminary evaluations tended to dismiss Ford as a historical accident, to describe his achievements as minor, and to consider him to have been largely

---

[16] Ibid.

inconsequential, if well meaning. Later ratings of Presidents tended to lump Ford into the Average/Low category meaning that he should be placed back in the pack, and trailing somewhat, along with the likes of Martin Van Buren, Benjamin Harrison and Millard Fillmore. Since the late 1990s the rankings have accorded Gerald Ford a higher position. Many Presidential scholars now place Ford in the Average/High category, which groups him among the likes of Dwight Eisenhower, Grover Cleveland and James Monroe. Some historians, notably Douglas Brinkley, claim that Ford should be ranked in the Good/Nearly Great category, however this generous assessment is rarely seconded. Ford rarely rates more than a passing mention in the general works of U.S. History and most of the basic studies of the 1970s clearly incline in the direction of the tumultuous Nixon Administration. At this point in time there is no historical consensus on Gerald Ford, and there is no way to know how future generations will remember him. The reevaluation of Ford's reputation is ongoing and will probably change over the decades to come.

When attempting to place Ford in historical perspective the historians, political scientists, journalists and interested parties must return to the personal side of his life. Ford was, at heart, a solid and steady Midwesterner. He lived the values of honesty and integrity taught by his parents. Ford was intelligent, but not brilliant, and he was utterly lacking in pretense. He did not care for opera, modern art, ballet, and other self-conscious "cultural" forms; moreover, he didn't care who knew it! Ford learned the virtues of hard work, diligence, and optimism growing up during the Great Depression and those qualities served him well through the lean years of the 1930s and throughout the course of World War II. Ford's basic decency and sense of connection with his peers showed itself when he won a surprising victory in the 1948 Congressional race, and during his years in the House of Representatives. He trusted his fellow politicos, possibly a little too much, and he was genuinely proud of saying that he had adversaries, but no enemies. Ford made very good, lifelong friends on both sides of the aisle during his quarter-century in Congress.

Ford served a brief period as the President of the United States. He was not in office long enough to have accomplished much of his agenda. Critics often charged that he had no agenda, and this was undoubtedly true to a point: Ford, a product of the non-ideological school of politics, chose not to think in absolutist terms and was willing to meet the opposition in a spirit of benevolence, and goodwill. In fact, Ford emerged as almost a perfect President for his times. Ford came into office following the upheaval of the Nixon years and the Viet Nam crucible and America badly needed "normalcy" in terms of a breathing space and time to gather herself. Ford's nice-guy image appealed to a country tiring of imperial Presidents, his apparently stable brood struck an agreeable note to a nation still wedded to a 1950s nuclear family ideal. His calm, but steady leadership style reassured many that the ship of state enjoyed capable direction at the helm.

In historical comparison Ford matches up fairly well with his immediate predecessors in office. He did not have the charisma of John F. Kennedy, nor, however, did he carry any Kennedy-like personal baggage. Ford, a straight arrow of renown, would never have approved of JFK's relentless amours, nor would he have kept a secret of severe back pain, other illnesses and possible addiction to painkilling drugs. Ford worked with Lyndon Johnson, and enjoyed a correct, if not friendly relationship with the thirty-sixth President. Ford took great offense at what he considered deception and double-dealing in his contacts with LBJ, the Lone Star Machiavelli. Ford placed a great premium on straight talk, and found Johnson to be inherently untrustworthy, much more so than an ordinary politician. Ford's integrity, bland though it may have been, put the minds of many politicians at ease in the sense that they generally believed what the President said, even if they didn't agree with his positions. Finally, Ford's steady and stable character measures up well when compared to the nearly clinical paranoia of Richard Nixon. Henry Kissinger said that a paranoid-schizophrenic only imagined that people were out to get him, and that a person (Nixon, in this case) who actually had enemies gunning for him was not really paranoid. While this may be true, it cannot be denied that Nixon's personal troubles, most of his own making, consumed his Administration, ruined many friends and subordinates, and plunged the nation into a needless and certainly unnecessary turmoil. Good old Jerry Ford, dull and predictable though he may have been, looks fine compared to his three immediate predecessors in the highest office in the land. As the President, Ford didn't please everybody, but no one questioned his essential character. He came into office playing a weak hand, but did well, given the circumstances.

Throughout his life Ford's solid character, shaped by family, community and patriotic values shone through ... and what a life it was! Ford lived an American success story; his biography resembled a Horatio Alger tale, come-to-life in the twentieth century. The son of an abused mother who fled across state lines to safety, a boy who grew up in the American heartland during the idyllic 1920s only to see them vanish into the grimness of the Great Depression, an Eagle Scout, a college football star, a college football coach who worked his way through Yale Law School, a male model, a war hero, a young attorney, a Congressman, the Vice-President of the United States, and, finally, the highest office in the land and most powerful figure on earth. Ford's life story reads like a movie script from Hollywood's Golden Age, except that every word of Gerald R. Ford's biography is true, not the brainchild of a scriptwriter. Gerald R. Ford lived a rich and full life, he quietly enjoyed triumphs and stoically endured tragedies, he built a reputation for honesty in a notoriously cutthroat profession, and he served his country honorably for nearly thirty years. Gerald R. Ford was the All-American President!

SELECTED BIBLIOGRAPHY

Baker, James A. *"Work Hard, Study ... And Keep Out of Politics!"* Adventures From an Unexpected Public Life. New York: Putnam, 2006.
Brinkley, Douglas. *Gerald R. Ford.* New York: Times Books, 2007.
Bush, George. *All The Best, George Bush*: My Life in Letters and Other Writings. New York: Scribner, 1999.
Cannon, James. *Time And Chance: Gerald Ford's Appointment With History*: 1913-1974. New York: HarperCollins, 1994.
Cannon, Lou. *Governor Reagan: His Rise to Power.* New York: PublicAffairs, 2003
Carson, Clarence. *A Basic History of the United States.* New York: American Textbook Committee, 1986.
DeFrank, Thomas. *Write It When I'm Gone: Remarkable Conversations With Gerald R. Ford.* New York: Penguin Publishing, 2007.
Edwards, Lee. *The Conservative Revolution: The Movement that Remade America.* New York: Simon & Schuster, 1999.
Ehrlichman, John D. *Witness To Power.* New York: Simon & Schuster, 1982.
Firestone, Bernard, and Alexy Ugrinsky (eds.) Gerald R. Ford and the Politics of Post-Watergate America. Westport, Connecticut: Greenwood Press, 1993.
Ford, Gerald R. *A Time To Heal: The Autobiography of Gerald R. Ford.* New York: Harper & Row, 1979.
Gaddis, John Lewis. *The Cold War: A New History.* New York: Penguin Publishing, 2005.
Gergen, David. *Eyewitness To Power.* New York: Simon & Schuster, 2000.
Greene, John Robert. *The Presidency of Gerald R. Ford.* Lawrence, Kansas: University of Kansas Press, 1995.

Hartmann, Robert T. *Palace Politics: An Inside Account of the Ford Years.* New York: McGraw-Hill, 1980.

Hayward, Steven F. *The Age of Reagan: The Fall of the Old Liberal Order, 1964-1980.* Roseville, California: Crown Publishing, 2001.

Horrocks, David A., and William H. McNitt, *Guide To Historical Materials In the Gerald R. Ford Library.* Ann Arbor, Michigan: Gerald R. Ford Library, 2003.

Johnson, Paul. *A History of the American People.* New York: HarperCollins, 1996.

Kissinger, Henry. *Ending The Vietnam War.* New York: Simon & Schuster, 2003.

Nessen, Ron. *It Sure Looks Different From The Inside.* Chicago: Playboy Press, 1978.

Nixon, Richard M. *RN: The Memoirs of Richard Nixon.* New York: Grosset & Dunlap, 1978.

Novak, Robert D. *The Prince of Darkness*: 50 Years of Reporting in Washington. New York: Crown Forum, 2007.

Patterson, James T. *Grand Expectations: The United States 1945-1974.* New York: Oxford University Press, 1995.

Phillips, Kevin P. *The Emerging Republican Majority.* New Rochelle, NY: Arlington House, 1969.

Reeves, Richard. A Ford, *Not A Lincoln.* New York: Harcourt, Brace & Jovanovich, 1975.

Rusher, William A. *The Rise of the Right.* New York: William Morrow & Company, 1984.

Schweikart, Larry and Michael Allen. *A Patriot's History of the United States.* New York: Penguin Group, 2004.

Schlesinger, Arthur M. Jr. *Journals:* 1952-2000. Penguin Group, 2008.

Taranto, James and Leonard Leo (eds.) Presidential Leadership: Rating the Best and the Worst in the White House. *New York: Wall Street Journal Books,* 2004.

Terhorst, Jerald F. *Gerald Ford and the Future of the Presidency.* New York: Third Press, 1974.

Tygiel, Jules *Ronald Reagan & The Triumph of American Conservatism.* New York: Longman-Pearson, 2005.

Vestal, Bud. Jerry *Ford, Up Close: An Investigative Biography.* New York: Coward, McCann, & Geoghegan, 1974

White, Theodore. *The Making of the President, 1972.* New York: Atheneum, 1973.

INDEX

A

Abraham, xv
abuse, 1, 81
academic difficulties, 17
access, 87
accommodations, 6
acquaintance, 3, 22, 37, 39, 40, 42, 113
Adams, John, xvi
Adams, John Quincy, xiv
adulthood, 5
adults, 7
Advice and Consent, xiv
Afghanistan, 111
Africa, 91, 111
African-American, 46
age, xvii, 2, 6, 40, 43, 44, 45, 52, 57, 114
agencies, xvii, 76
Air Force, 26, 90, 109, 112
alienation, 61, 111
ambassadors, xiv, 79
ambivalence, 72
American Presidency, 4, 11
appeasement, x, 92, 96, 100
apples, 14
armed conflict, 93
armed forces, 33
arms control, 91
arrest, 69
Arthur Krause, 9, 10

Arthur, Chester, xvi
Asia, 94
assassination, xvi, 54, 55, 88
assault, 25, 38
assessment, 117
assets, 71
athletes, 13
atmosphere, 15, 40, 54, 69, 73, 74, 77, 84, 91
authorities, 15
authority, 71

B

back pain, 118
backlash, ix, 81
baggage, 118
bail, 86
banking, 29
bankruptcy, 87
bargaining, 92
base, 31, 44, 70, 102
Belgium, 25
benefits, 73
Big-Man-On-Campus, 11, 46
blame, 86
blood, 54
bonds, 86
boxer, 15
boxing, 5, 14, 15, 16, 19, 30

breakdown, 66
breast cancer, 110
breathing, 117
Britain, 25, 27
brothers, 39
budding, 41
budget deficit, 86
burn, 104
Bush, George Herbert Walker, xvi
Bush, George W., xv
Bush, President George W., 116
buttons, 85

C

Cabinet, xiv, xvii
calculus, 10
caliber, 88
Cambodia, 65, 94
campaigns, 44
candidates, xiv, 29, 37, 49, 58, 61, 71, 73, 105, 106
Capitol Hill, 67, 73
Caribbean, 30
Carter, Jimmy, xvi, 72, 103, 105, 106, 107, 108, 111, 112, 113, 114, 116
cash, 69, 86
cattle, 6
caucuses, xiv
CBS, 89, 113
celebrity golf tournaments, 110
challenges, xix, 111
Chamber of Commerce, 68
character traits, xiii
Charles Manson, 88
charm, 41, 61
checks and balances, xiv
chemical, 111
Cheney, Dick, 107, 112, 116
Chicago, 11, 13, 26, 32, 39, 49, 60, 99, 122
Chief Justice, 54, 78
childhood, 4, 35
children, 41, 80
China, 32, 62, 91, 94
cities, 2, 46, 68, 73

citizens, 3, 80
citizenship, 10
City, xvii, 23, 48, 61, 74, 86, 87, 101
civil rights, 36, 49, 58, 59
civil rights establishment, 59
Civil War, 52
classes, 18, 19
cleaning, 6
Cleveland, Grover, xv, 117
climate, 3, 91
Clinton, William Jefferson, xvi
Clinton, William Jefferson (, xv
coaches, 9, 12, 17
Cold War, xvii, 49, 62, 91, 92, 95, 96, 121
collaboration, 115
collateral, 31, 71
college students, 67
colleges, 9, 17
Colonel Gene Tunney, 30
comedians, 1, 85
commercial, 26, 107
communication, 99
community, 7, 16, 25, 28, 35, 109, 118
compensation, 14, 110
competition, 11, 109
competitive sport, 5
complement, 30
composition, 66
comprehension, 55, 102
conditioning, 30
conference, 83, 89, 95, 114
conflict, 25, 58, 59
confrontation, 53
congestive heart failure, 116
Congress, xv, xvii, 1, 4, 16, 18, 26, 38, 42, 43, 44, 45, 46, 49, 52, 56, 57, 59, 62, 63, 68, 69, 70, 71, 72, 73, 75, 76, 79, 82, 84, 85, 86, 87, 92, 93, 95, 98, 109, 114, 115, 116, 117
consciousness, 4
consensus, ix, 12, 19, 51, 55, 76, 81, 83, 90, 117
consent, 19
conspiracy, 54, 70
constituents, 46, 70

Index

Constitution, xiii, xvii, 71, 76
constitutional law, xv
constitutional principles, xiv
consulting, 76
consumers, 85
consumption, 85
Continental, 6
controversial, 50, 71, 80, 84, 89, 95
convention, xv, 27, 48, 49, 60, 80, 101, 113
conversations, 75, 76
conviction, 25, 63, 92, 103
Coolidge, Calvin, xv
cooperation, 76
cost, 84, 94, 97, 103
counsel, xiv
courtship, 22, 24
covering, 76
credentials, 30, 42, 49, 62, 90
creep, 105
crises, xix
criticism, 57, 58, 59, 63, 81, 82, 110
cultural stereotypes, 3
currency, 79
customers, 9

D

dance, 39, 40
danger, 25, 93
Dean, John, 70
deduction, 18
deficit, 68, 86, 104, 107
delegates, xv, 95, 101, 112
Delta, 10
Delta Kappa Epsilon, 10
democracy, xv
Democrat, 42, 71, 98
Democratic Party, 60
demonstrations, 66
denial, 68
Denmark, 25
dentist, 36
Department of Justice, 76
depression, 110
depth, 111

detoxification, 111
dignity, 16, 111
diplomacy, xv, 91
disappointment, 49, 69, 104, 108
dissatisfaction, 58, 60
District of Columbia, 68, 111
domestic economy, 84
dominance, 56, 106
Dorothy Ayer Gardner King, 2
draft, 66
drawing, 16, 52, 60, 115
dream, 5, 45
drugs, 118
dumping, 48, 71

E

East Asia, 92
East China Sea, 32
Eastern Europe, 95, 98, 106
economic activity, 86
economic downturn, 9, 13
economic policy, 88, 113
economics, 10, 14, 35, 98
editors, 89
education, xi, xiii, 10, 94
Eisenhower Age, 51
Eisenhower, Dwight, 117
Eisenhower, Dwight D., xv, 45
Eisenhower, Dwight David, xvi
election, xiv, xv, 36, 37, 38, 44, 46, 48, 49,
  53, 55, 56, 58, 59, 60, 61, 62, 66, 67, 68,
  69, 75, 80, 84, 87, 101, 103, 104, 106,
  107, 108, 112
electoral coalition, 55
embargo, 84
emergency, xvii
emergency management, xvii
employers, 14
employment, 49, 98
encouragement, xi
enemies, 33, 44, 46, 60, 72, 73, 76, 117, 118
energy, 84, 100, 112
energy prices, 84
enforcement, 95

environment, 6, 46, 84
Equal Credit Opportunity Act, 85
Equal Rights Amendment, 89
equity, 85
ethnic groups, 95
Eugene Rostow, 21
Europe, 26, 95, 106
evacuation, 93, 94
evidence, 54, 70, 71, 74, 75, 76
exclusion, 10
execution, xiv, 94
Executive Order, xix
executive orders, 63
exercise, 44, 102
expenditures, 86, 87
expertise, 73

F

families, 15, 23
family life, 5, 24, 39
family members, 110
FBI, 88
fear, 37
fears, 56, 57
federal authorities, 71
Federal Bureau of Investigation, 76
federal government, 57, 59, 84
feelings, 39, 72, 89
Fifth Amendment, 71
Fillmore, Millard, xvi, 117
films, 99
financial, 9, 10, 26, 44, 52, 63, 81, 86, 110, 114
financial crisis, 86
financial sector, 26
fine arts, 3
Finland, 95
fires, 18, 32
fiscal conservative, 44
fitness, 30, 32
flexibility, 85, 91
flight, 91

football, 1, 5, 9, 10, 11, 12, 13, 14, 15, 18, 19, 21, 22, 23, 28, 31, 32, 40, 41, 42, 43, 46, 54, 104, 118
Football, 5
force, 27, 33, 38, 94, 95
Ford, Betty, 39, 41, 89, 109, 110, 111
Ford, Gerald Rudolph, 1
foreign affairs, 60, 91
foreign aid, 37, 44, 52
foreign policy, x, 27, 37, 38, 45, 90, 91, 92, 98, 100, 106
foundations, 24
France, 25
freedom, 27
friendship, 42, 48, 72, 113
fruits, 21
funds, 113

G

Gallup Poll, 107
Garfield, James, xvi
general election, 37, 38, 41, 45, 48, 53, 55, 56, 59, 61, 65, 67, 68, 103
genocide, 94
Georgia, xvi, 101, 103
Gerald Ford Presidential Museum, 113
Germany, 91
gifted, 4, 15
God, 105
government spending, 58, 65, 84, 85
governments, xvii, 91
governor, 41, 48, 60, 66, 70, 72, 80, 81, 88, 90, 98, 99, 103
grades, 18, 19
Grant, Ulysses S., xv
gravity, 85
Great Britain, 80
Great Depression, 1, 2, 6, 9, 10, 13, 14, 99, 117, 118
growth, xvii, 84, 86

Index

H

harassment, 76
Harrison, Benjamin, xvi, 117
Harrison, William Henry, xvi
Harvard Law School, 35
Hawaii, xix
Hayes, Rutherford B., xvi
health, 42, 59, 82, 115
height, 11, 72
heroism, 33
high school, 5
highways, 29
history, xiii, xix, 10, 51, 53, 67, 68, 71, 98, 111, 116
homes, 9, 11, 16
homework, 100
honesty, x, 4, 14, 79, 83, 117, 119
Hoover, Herbert, 113
Horatio Alger-novella, ix
hospitalization, 83
hostility, 72, 84
hotel, 32, 41, 88, 114
House, xv, xvii, 1, 4, 11, 42, 43, 45, 46, 47, 50, 52, 53, 54, 57, 58, 59, 61, 62, 63, 66, 68, 69, 70, 71, 72, 73, 75, 76, 81, 84, 90, 93, 114, 117, 122
House Minority Leader, 1, 58, 61, 62, 69, 71, 73
House of Representatives, xv, 1, 4, 11, 43, 46, 47, 58, 60, 63, 68, 69, 73, 75, 76, 84, 93, 115, 117
housing, 35
human, ix, 33, 111
Humphrey, Hubert, 60, 61, 66
hunting, 92
husband, 2, 3, 90

I

ideal, 118
ideals, 25
identity, 1, 25
ideology, 24, 43, 111
image, x, 2, 47, 87, 103, 105, 117
imagination, 73
immigrants, 3
immune system, 116
immunity, 71
impeachment, 63, 70, 75, 76, 77, 82, 114, 115
inauguration, 51, 69, 109
inauguration of President Carter, 109
income, 71, 110
independence, 93
individuals, xiii, 36, 90, 99
induction, 11
industries, 84
industry, 99
inflation, 10, 62, 79, 84, 85, 111
injuries, 13
inner ear, 4
innocence, 70
institutions, 9, 82
integrity, x, xiii, 79, 82, 83, 110, 117, 118
intellect, 15, 97
intelligence, 16, 106
interference, 95
Internal Revenue Service, 76
international diplomacy, 92
internationalism, 37
intervention, 111
invasions, 31
investment, 86
investment bank, 86
investors, 5
Iowa, 53, 99
Iran, 111, 113
Ireland, 31
iron, 116
Iron Curtain, 95
islands, 31
issues, xix, 24, 36, 44, 49, 54, 59, 60, 101, 103, 105

J

Jackson, Andrew, xv
Japan, 33, 36

Jefferson, Thomas, xv
Jews, 91
Johnson, Andrew, xvi
Johnson, Lyndon, 44, 57, 98, 103, 118
Johnson, Lyndon Baines, xv
Johnson, President Lyndon B., 53, 54, 55, 57, 59
journalists, 70, 103, 110, 117
Judiciary Committee, 75, 76, 84
jumping, 77

K

Kennedy family, 67
Kennedy, John F., xvi, 42, 49, 51, 53, 57, 115, 118
Kent County Republican Chairman, 36
Keynesian, 65
kill, 2
kinship, 3
Kissinger-Nixon foreign policy, x

L

labor relations, 49
landscape, 38
Laos, 65, 94
Latin America, 91
laws, xiii, 85
lead, 26, 27, 37, 59, 60, 69, 87, 89, 91, 96, 101, 107, 113
leadership, xiii, xix, 7, 27, 47, 51, 53, 56, 57, 62, 69, 92, 96, 110, 118
leadership style, 118
learning, 11, 15
legislation, xv, 44, 57, 87, 116
legs, 28
Leslie Lynch King, 2, 3, 6, 15, 18, 116
Liaison Office for Personnel Management, xvii
liberalism, 67
liberalization, 95
light, 30, 62, 69, 84
Lincoln, Abraham, xv

litigation, 81
loan guarantees, 86, 91
loans, 26, 87
lobbying, 73
love, xi, 15, 22, 23, 25, 39, 66
loyalty, 55, 62, 70, 83, 111
Lynette, 88

M

machinery, 39, 60, 66
Madison, James, xv
magnet, 3
magnitude, 68
majority, xv, 63, 66, 69, 82, 84, 101, 103, 105, 111
malfeasance, 70
man, ix, x, xvi, 1, 2, 4, 5, 6, 7, 15, 18, 22, 23, 24, 25, 27, 28, 37, 38, 39, 43, 47, 52, 53, 57, 58, 61, 62, 70, 72, 74, 80, 90, 104, 105, 113
manufacturing, 2
marijuana, 89
marketing, 40
marketplace, 62, 85
marriage, 1, 18, 24, 38, 39, 40, 41, 42, 79
Maryland, 61, 70
masculinity, 46
mass, 57
mass media, 57
materials, 43, 75
matter, 17, 23, 43, 60, 63, 69, 75, 82, 83, 89, 100, 107
McKinley, William, xv
media, 60, 63, 69, 81, 83, 95
membership, 4, 11, 36, 42
memory, x, 60
mental health, 83
mentor, 13, 27, 35, 36, 37, 75, 104
messages, 80
Mexico, 21, 116
Miami, 60
middle class, 5, 6, 13, 66
Middle East, 91

Index

military, xiii, xvi, 27, 30, 33, 35, 36, 37, 39, 93
military aid, 93
minimum wage, 44
mission, 93, 94
Missouri, 67, 73, 101, 103, 110
models, xix
momentum, 63, 101, 113
Monica Lewinsky affair, 114
Monroe, James, xv, 117
Moscow, 91
motels, 74
motivation, 36
murder, 54, 88
museums, 23

N

NAACP, 59
naming, xv, 19, 61, 90, 116
National Aeronautics and Space Administration, 44
National Economic Council, xviii
national emergency, xvii, 53
national period of mourning, 116
National Security Council, xvii
national ticket, 48, 108
natural gas, 6
negativity, 58
neglect, 28
negotiating, 56
Netherlands, 25
neutral, 33
New Deal, 25
New England, 14, 15, 23
New Hampshire primary, 101
nickel, 93
Nixon, Richard, xv, 43, 48, 62, 67, 68, 73, 82, 115, 118, 122
Nobel Prize, 100
nominee, 49, 55, 61, 68, 71, 98, 101, 105, 112, 114
Norway, 25
November 22, 1963, 53
nuclear family, 80, 118
nuclear weapons, 92

O

Oath of Affirmation, xiii
Obama, xvi
Obama, Barack, xvi
Office of Management and Budget, xviii
officials, xiv, 9, 32, 66, 87
oil, 6, 84, 85
Oklahoma, 71
openness, 89
operations, 30
opportunities, xix
optimism, 52, 117
organize, 43
organs, 82, 116

P

Pacific, 31, 32, 40, 116
pain, 18
Panama, 30, 101
paradigm shift, 55
paranoia, 118
parentage, 3
parents, ix, xi, 1, 2, 6, 15, 17, 18, 29, 32, 39, 117
participants, 33
payroll, 110
peace, 26, 27, 62, 91, 98, 103
pedigree, 48
permission, 19
personal choice, 72
personality, 24, 43, 46, 99
personality differences, 43
Philadelphia, 23, 27, 30, 105, 107
Philippines, xvi
phlebitis, 82
physical fitness, 30
physics, 10
Pierce, Franklin, xvi
platform, 48
plausibility, 75

playing, 5, 10, 11, 12, 13, 54, 59, 73, 75, 102, 118
pleasure, 17
PM, 78, 116
poison, 54
Poland, 25
police, 42, 69, 87
policy, xiv, xvii, 37, 45, 59, 62, 65, 73, 79, 90, 91, 92, 98, 105
policy initiative, 37
polio, 35
political damage, 71
political party, xv, xvi
political power, 28
politics, 3, 5, 25, 28, 36, 51, 54, 55, 58, 60, 62, 66, 67, 69, 77, 82, 98, 99, 102, 117
Polk, James K., xvi, 45
popular vote, xv, 50, 56, 61
population, 25, 26, 89
poverty, 110
pragmatism, 111
precedent, 105
preparation, 5, 19, 43, 94
preservation, 18
presidency, xiii, xiv, xvi, xvii, 63, 74, 82, 103, 113
President Clinton, 114, 115
President Nixon, 62, 63, 66, 69, 70, 71, 74, 76, 78, 81
press conferences, 57
prestige, xvii, 63, 83
primary school, 4, 40
probability, 77
professionals, 29, 68
proposition, 49
public affairs, 4
public life, x, xix, 5, 16, 22, 23, 36, 39, 59, 82, 98, 99, 102
public opinion, ix, xv, 25, 59, 70, 82, 94
public schools, 36
public service, xiii, 13, 24
pumps, 111
punishment, 83
purity, 60

Q

question mark, 103
questioning, 84

R

race, 37, 46, 52, 58, 59, 60, 61, 66, 101, 105, 108, 111, 117
radio, 25, 29, 53, 69, 99, 105
reading, 74
Reagan, Ronald, xv, 60, 66, 71, 72, 80, 90, 92, 95, 98, 99, 103, 107, 108, 111, 112, 115, 122
real estate, 29
reality, 25, 54, 73, 76, 106
reasoning, 49, 63, 83
recession, 47, 84, 85, 111
recognition, 5, 36, 95, 115
recreation, 5
recruiting, 9, 16, 19, 37
reform, 36, 37, 85
reformers, 29, 37
refugees, 93
rehabilitation, 111
rejection, 63
relief, 79, 102
Reorganization Act, xvii
reporters, 89, 112
Republican Congressional primary, 41
Republican Party, 25, 37, 46, 47, 52, 55, 56, 57, 59, 67, 74, 100
reputation, 7, 14, 16, 21, 25, 28, 32, 35, 44, 46, 47, 79, 82, 83, 99, 102, 110, 117, 119
resolution, 114
resources, 58
response, xix, 44, 70, 83, 86, 101
restaurants, 23
restrictions, 95
retirement, 109, 110, 111, 113
rewards, 70
rhetoric, 74
rights, 58, 59, 89
risk, 94

Index

Roosevelt, Franklin D., xv, xvii
Roosevelt, Theodore, xv, 25, 101
root, 87
roots, 11, 26, 42, 46, 49
rubber, 69
rules, 5
rural areas, 46

S

sadness, 77
safe haven, 94
safety, 94, 118
Saipan, 31
Saturday Night Live, 4, 97
savings, 6, 16
savings account, 6, 16
scholarship, xiii, 2, 9, 10
school, 3, 5, 6, 7, 9, 13, 15, 16, 17, 18, 19, 21, 22, 23, 24, 27, 30, 39, 40, 117
schooling, 4, 5
science, 15
Second World, 25
Secret Service, 76, 88, 89
securities, 35, 85
security, 110, 114
self-discipline, ix, 3, 4
semantics, 114
seminars, 113
Senate, xiv, 16, 21, 46, 50, 53, 57, 58, 63, 68, 69, 73, 84, 101, 114
Senator Eugene McCarthy, 59
services, 70, 87, 116
sexual intercourse, 89
sheep, 6
shock, 61
shoot, 23
shortage, 84
showing, 4, 13, 16, 18, 53, 68, 77, 84, 107
signals, 72
signs, 49, 65, 75, 84
slavery, 95
smoking, 76, 77
soccer, 92
social conservatives, 102

social organization, 7
social status, 48
social welfare, 62
society, 7, 11, 43, 52
solution, 35
South China Sea, 94
South Dakota, 67, 68, 88
Southeast Asia, 58, 59, 65, 93, 94, 97, 98
Soviet Union, x, 44, 53, 62, 91, 92, 98, 106
Soyuz, 91
specter, 82
speculation, 49
speech, 48, 49, 59, 74, 79, 85, 87, 93, 98, 101, 104, 107
spelling, 14
spending, 4, 39, 85, 86, 110
stability, 1
staff members, 62, 70
stagflation, 65
stars, 9, 12, 31
state, xv, 2, 5, 29, 37, 40, 41, 43, 46, 51, 56, 68, 71, 73, 83, 86, 87, 88, 93, 95, 99, 101, 108, 116, 118
state legislatures, xv
State of the Union address, xiv
states, xvi, 33, 56, 68, 73, 95, 99, 102, 103, 112
statistics, 108
stroke, 82
structure, 16, 55
style, 2, 3, 54, 82, 88, 103, 105, 106, 111
subgroups, 49
succession, 71
summer program, 18
Sun, 41
supervisor, 19
Supreme Court, xiv, 21, 54, 63, 76, 77, 78, 89
Supreme Court nominee, 63
survivors, 33
sympathy, 55, 82
syndrome, 110

Index

T

tactics, 59
Taft, William Howard, xvi, 101
takeover, 66
talent, x, 21, 67
target, 37
tax evasion, 70
tax increase, 87
tax reform, 85
taxes, 70, 85
team sports, 4
teams, 13, 16
technology, xviii, 91
Telecommunications Adviser, xvii
telephone, 100, 116
temperament, 63
tension, 58, 67
tensions, 91, 95
tenure, 89
territory, 37, 93, 101
testing, 30, 56
Tomahawk Cruise Missile, 92
tonic, 18
trade, 16, 56, 89, 91
training, 12, 15, 30, 32, 33, 99
transactions, 35
transcripts, 77
translation, 91
transport, 116
Treasury, 71, 72, 86, 87
Treasury Secretary, 71, 72, 86, 87
treaties, 101
treatment, 52, 93, 111
trial, 19, 83, 114
Truman, Harry S., xv
Truman, President Harry S., 110
tuition, 10
turnout, 68
Tyler, John, xvi

U

United States (USA), ix, xiii, xv, xix, 1, 2, 3, 6, 15, 26, 29, 33, 35, 45, 46, 48, 62, 65, 70, 71, 73, 76, 77, 78, 79, 81, 86, 91, 92, 94, 95, 96, 97, 100, 104, 106, 108, 110, 111, 117, 118, 121, 122
universities, 15
university education, 9
University of Michigan, 2, 7, 9, 10, 13, 14, 18, 27, 41, 104, 108, 113
urban, 38, 87, 107
urban areas, 38

V

Van Buren, Martin, xvi, 117
vein, 1, 85
veto, xiv, 45, 72, 84, 86
Vice President, xviii, 1
vice-presidency, xvi
Vietnam, 59, 61, 62, 65, 92, 93, 94, 96, 122
violence, 66
vision, 1, 57, 96, 104
visions, 58
Vladivostok, 92
volunteer work, 41
vote, xv, 14, 38, 44, 46, 53, 57, 58, 61, 73, 75, 86, 87, 101, 103, 106, 107, 115
voters, 46, 49, 68, 84
voting, xiv, xv, xvi, 49, 67, 69, 73, 98
voting majority, xiv
voting record, 49, 98

W

Wallace, George, 60, 61, 66
war, 25, 26, 27, 29, 30, 31, 32, 33, 35, 39, 45, 59, 61, 65, 66, 93, 118
war hero, 45, 118
war years, 30
Warren, Earl, 54

Index

Washington, xiv, xv, 4, 32, 33, 42, 43, 66, 67, 68, 69, 73, 77, 79, 82, 84, 88, 92, 94, 107, 109, 110, 115, 116, 122
Washington, George, xiv, xv, 33
water, 32, 33
Watergate, 63, 68, 69, 70, 74, 75, 76, 77, 79, 84, 121
weakness, 67, 84, 102
wealth, 48, 81
welfare, 32, 85
White House, x, xvii, 27, 42, 48, 55, 59, 61, 62, 67, 69, 70, 72, 74, 75, 77, 79, 80, 81, 82, 86, 90, 93, 95, 100, 104, 107, 109, 114, 122
WHO, xvii, 98
wildlife, 18
Wilson, Woodrow, xv
Wisconsin, 16, 45, 53, 73, 103
withdrawal, 94
wool, 45
work ethic, 3, 17, 19
working class, 13
workload, 19
World War I, xvii, 1, 27, 33, 40, 67, 91, 95, 116, 117
worldview, 100
worry, 39, 70
wrongdoing, 74, 79

Y

Yale Law School, 14, 16, 17, 18, 19, 21, 22, 26, 29, 118
Yale University, 14, 16, 40

Z

Zachary Taylor, xvi